THE BATTLE OF TOTOPOTOMOY CREEK

THE BATTLE OF TOTOPOTOMOY CREEK

Polegreen Church and the Prelude to Cold Harbor

ROBERT BLUFORD JR.

Charleston   London

THE
History
PRESS

Published by The History Press
Charleston, SC 29403
www.historypress.net

Front cover: Federal general Winfield Scott Hancock with division commanders (left to right) Francis Channing Barlow, David Bell Birney and John Gibbon. Petersburg, Virginia. *Courtesy of the Library of Congress*.
Back cover, inset: View of the Shelton House near Totopotomoy Creek in Virginia. Revolutionary War patriot Patrick Henry was reportedly married in the parlor of this house. This house was also at the center of the Battle of Totopotomoy Creek during the American Civil War. *Photo by Rob Shenk. Courtesy of Wikimedia Commons*.

First published 2014

Manufactured in the United States

ISBN 978.1.62619.251.5

Library of Congress CIP data applied for.

Contents

Acknowledgements

I wish to express my profound appreciation to Dr. Edwin C. Bearss for his contributions to the manuscript on which this book is based. He kindly spent hours of his time and energy reading the text—not once, but twice—for accuracy and commented on my work. Dr. Bearss has few, if any, peers in his knowledge of the Civil War and is a world-known lecturer on the topic. He bears the title of chief historian emeritus of the National Park Service.

To my granddaughter Michelle, who transitioned this project from years of handwritten and manually typed notes into modern technology, goes a heartfelt thank-you for breathing life into this book.

Chapter 1

Polegreen Church

Polegreen Church was not just another old church. There are many old
churches in the South, and a lot of them have bloodstained floors from
being used as hospitals by both the Federals and Confederates during the
Civil War. Polegreen was a special church and had been for more than a
century before the war. It was special because it was the center of energy in
the struggle for civil and religious liberty in colonial Virginia and because it
was the church of Samuel Davies, the great "dissenter" and a minister of
the gospel who gave more credibility to the Great Awakening in eighteenth-
century Virginia than any other leader. He had no peer in terms of religious
influence in colonial Virginia or perhaps even in colonial America.

Virginia's General Assembly was the first legislative body in the world to
adopt a statute guaranteeing religious freedom to all its citizens. Thomas
Jefferson and James Madison were the framers of the U.S. Bill of Rights,
which was adopted in 1791, the first article of which was the same guarantee
already granted to Virginians. These two political giants, Jefferson and
Madison, have rightfully been given credit for their contribution to
our Constitution and to our heritage. What is generally unknown, or
unrecognized, is the half century of struggle for these freedoms that preceded
the ratification of the Constitution. In particular, little is currently known of
the enormous contribution to the struggle for these freedoms that was made
by Samuel Davies. At the present time, considerable effort is being made to
establish an appropriate memorial to Davies on the site where he began his
exceptional work and founded Polegreen Church in 1748. This site has been

registered as a historic landmark by the Department of Historic Resources of the commonwealth of Virginia and has also been placed on the National Register of Historic Places by the Department of the Interior. Without Samuel Davies, Polegreen may never have become a church and certainly would not have gained the renown it had in the middle of the 1700s. What immediately follows is a brief sketch of Davies and Polegreen.

Samuel Davies was born in 1723 in St. Georges, Delaware, the only son of Welsh parents. His mother, a devout Christian, had great difficulty in conceiving and, at his birth, named him after the biblical Samuel, meaning "God's gift." He was never a robust child. When, in his early teens, he sensed he was being called by God to be a minister, he went to a "log college" operated by Samuel Blair in Faggs Manor, Pennsylvania. This was in the day when formal education at a higher level was a rarity. Davies proved to be a diligent and brilliant student, though at the price of his health. When he finished his formal education at twenty-three years of age, he had tuberculosis.

It is essential to have an understanding of at least some dimensions of the situation into which Samuel Davies and the Presbyterian dissenters of Hanover County injected themselves. Certain social dynamics of the first half of the eighteenth century form the backdrop against which the struggle for religious freedom took place: the spiritual poverty of the church presided over by the Anglican priesthood, the beginning of the Great Awakening, the plight of the imported slaves and their descendants, the condition of the white indentured servants brought into the colony in large numbers, the strict control of religious expression (particularly in the Tidewater region) and the dwindling credibility of the Anglican priests themselves. This list could go on and on, but there are enough ingredients here noted to say that the situation in general was ripe for something explosive. Stated simply, the ties between the colonial government and its official religious institution, the Anglican Church, were about to unravel.

In 1983, the Pulitzer Prize for History was awarded to Rhyss Isaac for his volume *The Transformation of Virginia, 1740–1790*. This Australian, after ten years of research on eighteenth-century Virginia history, made some fascinating observations about the role of religion in contributing to the mood and substance of the American Revolution. A few sentences help illuminate those times:

> *Social disquiet was arising in Virginia by mid-century from a variety*
> *of causes, but the most dramatic signs of change appeared in the sphere*

Samuel Davies, Presbyterian educator. *Courtesy of Wikimedia Commons.*

*of religion. A movement of dissent from the Church of England itself
was commencing in the 1740's* [sic]. *In some places, common people
were departing from the established churches into congregations of
their own making. The parish community at the base of the barely
consolidated traditional order was beginning to fracture. The rise of
dissent represented a serious threat to the system of authority. The
nature and extent of the anxiety produced in Virginia by the Great
Awakening—that astonishing revival that reached every region of
colonial America—must be examined before we can understand the
sudden intensification of anticlericalism.*

*The first signs of the coming disturbance in traditionally Anglican parts
of Virginia appeared in Hanover County in about 1743, when numbers
of ordinary people led by Samuel Morris, a "Bricklayer," began readings
from George Whitefield's sermons.* [Whitefield, the great evangelical
preacher and breakaway assistant of John Wesley, had preached
in Williamsburg in 1739, during his first tour of the colonies.]
*The pious gatherings soon reached such a size that a meetinghouse was
built to accommodate them. Disaffection from the Church seems to have
been sufficiently general that "when the Report of these Sermons and the
Effects occasioned by reading them was spread Abroad," Samuel Morris
was invited to travel and conduct meetings "at a considerable Distance."
The movement took a new direction in the middle of 1743 when emissaries
from Hanover persuaded the Reverend William Robinson, a New Side
Presbyterian missionary among the Scotch-Irish in southwest Virginia, to
come and preach. From then on, the Hanover group identified themselves
as Presbyterians, rather than Anglicans, and periodic visits from revivalist
preachers occasioned mass meetings that created considerable commotion.*

Four years later, Samuel Davies, twenty-three years old and friend
of the then deceased William Robinson, responded to the invitation of
Samuel Morris and friends to come be their spiritual leader. He first went
to Williamsburg and obtained from Governor William Gooch a license
to preach in three locations in Hanover County and one in Henrico—all
named Morris Reading House. He remained only six weeks and returned
to Delaware a physically ill man. Three months later, his wife and infant
son died, and Davies, ill with consumption, remained through the winter
of 1747–48. Still not well, but desiring to die working rather than waiting,
he returned to Hanover County and, with improved health, continued his
remarkable work for eleven years.

He was a man of exceptional gifts. Shortly after his arrival, word spread quickly throughout the area concerning his teaching and preaching. The response was dramatic; hundreds came not only to Polegreen but also to the other preaching points established by the dissenters in Hanover, Henrico, Louisa, Goochland and Caroline Counties. He was asked to come preach in Cumberland County and founded a church there in 1754. In 1755, he founded Briery Church in what is now Charlotte County. He labored with a compassion and zeal, coupled with a keen intellect and pastoral concern that has rarely been equaled and perhaps never exceeded in the commonwealth of Virginia.

Davies's base of ministry was at Polegreen, first called a reading house, then a meetinghouse and finally a church, built by brick mason Samuel Morris. The changing name of the place of worship reflects the evolving credibility of the Presbyterian dissenters. The dimensions of the struggle for religious freedom in Virginia, and ultimately in the colonies as a whole, were being defined in the contest between the Presbyterians in Hanover County, led by Samuel Davies, and the colonial government in Williamsburg. What took place in the next three decades between the Baptists, followed by the Methodists, and the Virginia governor and burgesses are extensions and sometimes exaggerations of what was shaping up in the fourth and fifth decades of the eighteenth century at Polegreen.

Davies's perception of his personal ministry and that of the Christian church compelled him to address the intellectual and spiritual needs of more than just white colonists. He founded the Society for Managing the Missions and Schools among the Indians, yet it was the response of the black slaves to Davies's ministry that was extraordinary. At a time when educating slaves was unthinkable, even frightening to some, Davies was teaching them to read and write. The reward for that accomplishment was the gift of a Bible or Isaac Watts's *Psalms and Hymns*, which Davies had begged from friends in Great Britain. The slaves would gather in Davies's home at night to learn and help one another. He wrote to a friend of their participation at Polegreen:

> *Never have I been so struck with the appearance of an assembly, as when I have glanced my eye to that part of the Meeting House where they usually sit, adorned, for so it seemed to me, with so many black countenances eagerly attentive to every word they hear, and frequently bathed in tears. A considerable number, (about an hundred) have been baptized, after a proper time for instruction.*

Davies reported that forty African American slaves partook of communion on one Sunday.

By 1755, Davies had persuaded five more Presbyterian ministers to join him in the work of ministry east of the Blue Ridge. He successfully petitioned the Synod of New York to establish a new Presbytery, the first south of the Potomac. It was founded in December 1755 at the Polegreen site and appropriately was named Hanover Presbytery. Reflecting the deep concern of the new church's governing body as the storm clouds of the French and Indian War were gathering, the first business was to set a day of fasting and prayer "on account of the present critical and alarming state of Great Britain and the British plantations in America." Hanover Presbytery became the founding body of Presbyterianism in the South and into the far Southwest.

Davies not only had a noticeable impact on the religious scene in mid-eighteenth-century Virginia, which, as Rhyss Isaac has so well documented, in turn contributed greatly to the American Revolution, but also made a marked impression on one of the heroes of that Revolution—Patrick Henry.

When Samuel Davies arrived in Hanover County in 1747, Patrick Henry was eleven years old. Patrick's home was at Studley, four miles east of Polegreen Church. This was in the same area where Haw's Shop was later built and where the Civil War battle of that name occurred. Patrick had been named after his uncle, an Anglican priest, whose church, St. Paul's Parish, was five miles farther east in Hanover County at Old Church, which was a military site during the Civil War. Young Patrick's mother was impressed with the ministry of Davies, joined Polegreen Church and was joined by her son in attendance at worship throughout his adolescence and until he was twenty-two years old. While he apparently never joined up with the Presbyterian dissenters, Patrick was influenced significantly by Davies, who was credited by Patrick with "having taught me what an orator should be." One study concludes that Patrick Henry not only was influenced by the substance of Davies's preaching but also emulated Davies's style of speaking.

Davies was in constant demand as a preacher and covered on horseback a remarkably large "parish." He founded churches in Hanover, Caroline, Henrico, Louisa, Cumberland, Goochland and Prince Edward Counties. He was also a friend and contemporary of Jonathan Edwards, leader in New England of the Great Awakening. He was invited by Edwards to share in his ministry in New England. One hundred years after Davies's death, his sermons were being reprinted, sold and read more than any of his contemporaries, who include the likes of Jonathan Edwards, Gilbert Tennent, John and Charles Wesley and George Whitefield. Indicative of

Davies's stature as a pulpiteer is that, in 1993, his three volumes of sermons were republished.

In spite of the demands on his energies during his extensive ministry in and beyond Polegreen Church, Davies found or made time to exercise other gifts. Having introduced the singing of hymns in worship in his several congregations, he became the first American-born hymn writer. He is credited with writing many hymns, which were first published in Great Britain and used by Baptists, Methodists and Lutherans, as well as Presbyterians, during the Great Awakening. As late as the mid-nineteenth century, fourteen of his hymns were still being sung in worship by the Methodist denomination, and some were sung as late as the twentieth century.

Davies was deeply moved by the plight of slaves. He was drawn to them and they to him. They no doubt inspired him in his hymn writing. He wrote to a friend in England of their presence in his home in the evenings:

> *Sundry of them lodged all night in my kitchen, and sometimes when I awoke about two or three o'clock in the morning, a torrent of sacred harmony poured into my chamber, and carried my mind away into heaven. In this seraphic exercise, some of them spend almost the whole night. I wish, sir, you and their other benefactors could hear any of these sacred concerts. I am persuaded it would surprise and please you more than an Oratorio, or a St. Cecilia's Day.*

Davies's talent for writing hymns was likely related to his gifts as a poet. In 1751, some of his poetry was published in Williamsburg, and it was widely read throughout Virginia and the other colonies, as well as in Great Britain.

Samuel Davies, both by his personal example and by his efforts, drew attention to the cherished value of Presbyterians in developing an educated clergy. He believed that ministerial education should embody the best in classical subjects, not merely theology. He felt the great need for qualified and competent ministers in the Virginia colony, and as there was no institution ready to train non-Anglicans, he gave his energy to support the fledgling College of New Jersey, later to become Princeton University. The College of New Jersey had begun the same year Davies came to Hanover County. Its leaders and its founding governing body, the Synod of New York, persuaded Davies to go to England in 1753 to raise funds for the college. In so doing, he built upon his reputation as a pulpit orator in the colony and soon was in demand as a speaker in Scotland and England. His sermons were first published in England, and a century later were still being widely read there.

He was successful in his fundraising efforts in England. Nassau Hall, Princeton University's first permanent building, was built with money he generated. Without doubt, Davies sowed the seeds in Hanover Presbytery for the building of a college in Virginia twenty years later—Hampden-Sydney, which, when organized, adopted the curriculum of Princeton. Davies's personal friendships with and/or direct influence on the founders of Hampden-Sydney are notable. His Hanover assistant in 1752, John Todd, became a principal leader in the new college's development, along with men such as Samuel Stanhope Smith, Patrick Henry, James Madison, Colonel William Cabell and Colonel John Morton. Clarence Bradshaw, in his *History of Hampden-Sydney College*, gives due credit to Davies and those whom he attracted to the Virginia Colony to serve as ministers for laying the foundation for Hampden-Sydney, the second-oldest institution of higher learning in the South, following only the College of William and Mary.

His trip to England with Gilbert Tennent in 1753–54, at the cost of being separated from his family in Hanover County, underlined his commitment to the education of youth at the highest level. In 1758, the College of New Jersey called Davies to be its president. He was torn between two loves—Princeton and the Hanover ministry. Unable to make the decision, he asked Hanover Presbytery to make it, and it decided he should remain at Polegreen. A year later, the call was renewed, and with genuine anguish at leaving his only parish ministry, he left Hanover for Princeton. His presidency lasted only eighteen months. He fell ill with fever, and the primitive medical procedure of bleeding the patient was employed. Infection ensued, and Samuel Davies died on February 4, 1761, not having yet reached his thirty-eighth birthday.

The achievements of Samuel Davies are extraordinary, his youth notwithstanding. His contributions to one of the most precious freedoms cherished by the citizens of our land are without question. His biographer, George William Pilcher, writes:

> *Thus it was that a generally relaxed attitude toward the dissenters had come to prevail in the colony during the latter part of Samuel Davies' residence in Hanover. In reality, the dissenters acquired more freedom than they asked for, some of them being allowed to preach unmolested wherever they desired until the Revolution. In fact, as early as 1755, more than three years before Davies left Hanover, John Wright reported that he could even then: "Preach anywhere, being so distant from the metropolis, and the time being so dangerous and shocking." This relative freedom, fostered so effectively by Davies, was to continue even through the Revolution and*

the chaotic days immediately following independence. Once the new state legislature was established, it was besieged with petitions and memorials signed by dissenters of all denominations, opposing the continuance of a government-supported church. The Hanover Presbytery persisted in its leadership of this opposition throughout the period. Its ablest spokesman, the Reverend John B. Smith, president of Hampden-Sydney College, addressed a legislative committee for three full days, arguing against a bill for government support of religion. Furthermore, Smith was instrumental in winning the eventual passage of the act establishing religious freedom in Virginia, an act that served the framers of the Constitution in guaranteeing freedom of worship. An early nineteenth-century historian, William Henry Foote, maintained that "It is owing to the exertions made by Davies, and the public discussions on this subject, in which a man of his powers engaged, that sentiments, so just and liberal respecting religious liberty, have pervaded the population of Virginia."

Polegreen Church became the dynamic base from which Davies operated. In a war in which irony and paradox were commonplace, another strange set of circumstances surrounds the story of the erection and the destruction of Polegreen Church. In 1755, the rapidly growing congregation of Presbyterians, in response to the dynamic and eloquent Samuel Davies, built a new and larger sanctuary to accommodate the crowds who came to hear him preach. Even then, in pleasant weather, the building proved to be too small, and worship services were held outdoors "in the grove." A little more than a century later, this same place of worship was destroyed in a war during which the Confederate states were presided over by a close kinsman of Samuel Davies, President Jefferson Davis.

The kinship of these two men is well documented. The Welsh family who came to America spelled the family name "David," ending with a *d*. They had at least two male children, David and John, both of whom at various times spelled their surname "Davis" and "Davies." David and Martha Davies were the parents of Samuel. John and Ann Davis were the parents of Evan Davis. Thus, Samuel Davies and Evan Davis were first cousins. In 1755, the year Polegreen Church was built, Evan fathered a son whom he named after his now famous preacher cousin, Samuel Davies. This Samuel Davis became the father of Confederate president Jefferson Davis.

In the midst of the French and Indian War, Polegreen Church was built. The nation had not yet been born. It was still twenty-one years before the Declaration of Independence, twenty-six years before Yorktown and victory, thirty-six years before the adoption of the Bill of Rights. By then, Polegreen Church had stood as a symbol of the struggle for civil and religious liberty for more than a century. Now, in 1864, it was to go down in flames in that most tragic and destructive of all wars in which the nation has fought. Though they were separated in time by a century and the many changes that came about over that period, the beginning and the end of Polegreen Church knew the presence of kinsmen Samuel Davies and Jefferson Davis.

Chapter 2

1862

The first casualty of the Civil War occurred before the firing on Fort Sumter. The battleground was in the hearts of unreasonable and unbending human beings. The first casualty was reason itself. If only those on both sides of the battle line could have had a glimpse of Malvern Hill, Antietam, Fredericksburg, Gettysburg, the Wilderness, Spotsylvania, Cold Harbor, Petersburg and scores of other engagements that, after four years, left 621,000 dead and an equal number maimed for life, it all might have been averted. But reason did not prevail, and the legacy of that awful time in our country's life still haunts and hurts.

The record of the year 1861 reveals a nation as a whole that did not, or could not, know what it was getting into. In many quarters, there was a festive atmosphere, as revealed at First Manassas, when people drove buggies from Washington to enjoy the contest with food and drink on hand. A member of the Richmond Howitzer Artillery vividly described Richmond's entry into the war:

In April, 1861, to the charming quiet life that Richmond had so long been leading, a sudden standstill was put. An unexpected crisis confronted the city in a twinkling, and called for instant decision. Throughout the preceding winter the most animated discussions in regard to the secession of the South from the Union had been held in the Capitol, the press, the streets, and the homes; the political condition was extremely threatening, but Richmond did not want to see the Union broken; did all it could to prevent the occurrence, and sincerely cherished the hope that it would not be—that the clouds would roll by, the storm not burst. This hope, illusive in reality, was held to amidst all the sharp, bitter contentions at home, despite all the insulting menaces and mockeries hurled across the border by the enemy that was soon to cross it in arms.

The Convention, specially called to pass upon the grave subject of secession, sat daily in the Capitol, and the citizens were absorbed in its debates, though business went on as usual; the city looked bright and attractive, the streets resounded with the cry of the melodious "charcoal" hucksters, who seemed at least to be ubiquitous, and the fine, balmy weather plentifully brought out the buds and flowers of spring. All at once came news of Beauregard's firing upon Fort Sumter; hope nearly vanished. A few days after, simultaneously with the news of Lincoln's calling out seventy-five thousand troops, sped Richmond's resolution to secede, and the Convention, hesitating no longer, passed the ordinance of secession. The die was cast—war had come after all. Stirred with the deepest feeling, resolutely, heartily, exhibiting only a proper enthusiasm, the city began to gird itself for its share in the brunt of the decreed contest. It was almost a race with the young men to see who would buckle on armor first and enlist for a war which was destined to be the bloodiest and longest since the fall of Napoleon at Waterloo, though inexperience led nearly all to believe that it was going to be a picnic, or a sort of picnic affair.

In the South, for the very exceptional few who could afford it, army duty might include having one's body servant taking care of personal and menial duties while in camp.

The war had been going on for some months before the harsh realities began to sink in on both sides; but by then, it was too late to undo the mischief. The ill-equipped and untrained army of the Confederacy was locked into a life-and-death struggle with a vastly superior force with comparatively endless resources of men and equipment. A breakaway section of the country, with a population totaling 9 million, was defending itself against the balance with a population of 22 million and most of the nation's industry. The leadership in the North, both civil and military, saw the South as an easy pushover, predicting victory in three to four weeks. The South, bolstered by the conviction that the North had exceeded its constitutionally undefined and previously untested legal right to militarily invade a sovereign state for the purpose of maintaining a union by force, fought a war mostly by sheer heart and courage in defense of home and hearth. The idea of quick victory soon vanished. Four weeks turned into four terrible years.

By the late winter of 1862, Robert E. Lee had been ordered by Jefferson Davis to relinquish command of Confederate forces charged with defense of South Carolina, South Georgia and East Florida and come to Richmond. During the spring, Major General George B. McClellan, leading an army of 100,000 men, had pushed up the peninsula almost to the outskirts of Richmond. The capital of Virginia had taken on a new title, the capital of the Confederacy. As such, it was understandably the prime target of the armies of the North.

From McClellan's observation balloons ten miles northeast of Richmond, the city of thirty-eight thousand citizens, virtually in its entirety, could be seen. Following much political maneuvering between Jefferson Davis and the Confederate congress, Lee was charged "with the conduct of military operations for the armies of the Confederacy." This he did for nearly three months, when, on June 1, he was made commander of the Army of Northern Virginia, taking the place of General Joseph E. Johnston, who had been wounded at Seven Pines. June 1 was a day to be remembered by those who loved and appreciated the old church in Hanover County. Exactly two years later, Polegreen Church was to be added to the long list of war casualties.

The situation east of Richmond was extremely serious. McClellan had divided his much larger force into two fighting units. His right wing he retained north of the Chickahominy and pushed it north/northwest, ten miles to Mechanicsville in Hanover County.

Lee inherited an army from Johnston that lacked discipline in the lower ranks and whose commanders had not yet seen the value of a mound of dirt (rather than a human body) absorbing a Minié ball. Not without criticism within the ranks and from elements of the press was Lee able to gain a victory among his own troops and convince them of the wisdom of preparing fortifications. The press dubbed him "the king of spades" for his insistence on digging rifle pits and breastworks. By mid-June, the eastern defense of Richmond was reasonably secured, so much so that Lee turned his attention to what was going on in Hanover County around Mechanicsville. It now seemed evident to him that McClellan intended first to link up with Union troops marching south from Fredericksburg and then invest the Confederate capital with soldiers closing in on the city's eastern approaches. What Lee needed badly was some accurate military intelligence of the enemy's movement. In particular, he needed to know how deeply into Hanover County McClellan's right wing extended. To learn this, he called on the dashing twenty-nine-year-old Brigadier General J.E.B. Stuart. Lee desired all the information he could get, but he may have been a bit surprised by Stuart's suggestion that he might ride completely around the Federals massed in eastern Henrico and Hanover Counties. Lee cautioned Stuart not to take any unreasonable risks, adding that the intelligence Stuart could gather would be useful in further operations; in particular, he asked that Stuart take note of the watershed of the Totopotomoy. This information was to be more critical two years in the future than at that moment.

The famous cavalry ride of J.E.B. Stuart and his 1,200 troops on June 12–15, 1862, encircling McClellan's army, is well known. It is mentioned here because it confirmed the route Major General Thomas J. "Stonewall" Jackson was to take in a fortnight, when he marched in from the valley of Virginia to join the left flank of Lee's army at Mechanicsville. The route from Hanover Courthouse to Mechanicsville passed then, and still does, by the Polegreen Church site. Lee's orders to Stuart concerning the disposition of McClellan's forces specifically mentioned recording the topographical characteristics of the Totopotomoy Creek watershed.

Polegreen Church was situated in a piece of woods sixty feet east of the Hanover Courthouse–Mechanicsville Road, shown on military maps of the time as the Cold Harbor Road. The church also lay three-tenths of a mile south of Totopotomoy Creek. The Totopotomoy had been named to honor an Indian chief who had taken the side of white settlers and was slain during a battle with Native Americans along this creek in 1656. The creek's headwaters begin about twenty-five miles from the point where it enters the Pamunkey River. Its head and mouth are on almost the same latitude. Its course on a map resembles a shallow bowl. The area that Jackson crossed in June 1862 and that, for several days, was the focal point of U.S. Grant's offensive move toward Richmond in 1864 is a swampy section about fifty yards wide that gives way to bluffs, which rise about seventy-five feet. The swampland continues for several miles, and it played a prominent part in the defense of the Confederate capital in 1864.

In midafternoon on June 23, Jackson and one courier rode toward Richmond from Louisa County on his line of march from the Shenandoah Valley. He had been secretly summoned by Lee to meet and plan for the defense of Richmond. He made his way to the widow Dabbs's house, east of Richmond, where Lee had established his headquarters about halfway between the city and McClellan at Seven Pines. The council of war was attended by Major Generals D.H. Hill, A.P. Hill and Longstreet, all of whom assumed that Jackson, until he walked through the door, was 110 miles to the west. The meeting ended after about four hours, and Jackson and his courier were back in the saddle for an all-night return ride to his

Map of the American Civil War battlefield at Totopotomoy and Cold Harbor with the position on May 26, 1864. *Courtesy of Wikimedia Commons.*

command. Jackson's forces were already moving along the Virginia Central Railroad. The decision had been made. Jackson would take up a position from which he could launch a flanking attack on Brigadier General Fitz John Porter's Fifth Corps, which was the right wing of McClellan's army north of the Chickahominy.

Lee issued a general order on June 24 in the expectation that there would be no uncertainty as to each commander's role. In this, he was not entirely successful. While the Seven Days Battles ended in victory for the Army of Northern Virginia, that victory might have ended in a total defeat of McClellan's Army of the Potomac and certainly with fewer Confederate casualties if there had been greater coordination by Lee's lieutenants—the Hills, Longstreet and Jackson. In his general order, Lee had stated, "At 3 o'clock Thursday morning, 26th instant, General Jackson will advance on the road leading to PoleGreen church, communicating his march to General Branch."

Lee had ordered Stuart, with his 1,800 cavalrymen, to leave Richmond on the twenty-fifth, meet Jackson in Ashland and cover his left on the way to the encounter at Mechanicsville. These horsemen, along with Jackson's wing of 18,500, were strung out for fifteen miles along the Hanover Courthouse–Cold Harbor Road that passes Polegreen. Lee had expected them to be gathered as a fighting force on the plateau on which Polegreen stands by the afternoon of the twenty-sixth, ready to be the flanking force against General Porter's forces on the right of McClellan's army, as A.P. Hill's division threatened Mechanicsville—three and a half miles southwest of Polegreen.

One of Jackson's artillerymen later wrote, "Our destination was now evident. The army around Richmond was waiting for Jackson to dislodge McClellan from the Chickahominy swamp, and our attack was to be made on his right flank. It seems our powers of endurance had been over-estimated, or the distance miscalculated, as the initiatory battle at Mechanicsville was fought by A.P. Hill without Jackson's aid."

As Jackson marched down the road from Hanover Courthouse toward Mechanicsville, A.P. Hill, impatient at Jackson's failure to arrive as planned and coordinate with him on the attack on Porter, launched his attack without having established contact with Jackson, who was still north of the Totopotomoy. When the troops from the valley arrived at the creek, they found that the Federal pickets had destroyed a part of the bridge, which was three-tenths of a mile from Polegreen Church. Captain R.J. Harding, one of Hood's Texas–Georgia–South Carolina Brigade, described the situation the Confederates encountered at the river crossing:

> *Arriving at this creek about the middle of the afternoon, the Texas skirmishers (I was one of them myself and so speak from personal knowledge) discovered that the bridge across was in flames and that a considerable force of the Federals on the farther bank from us was doing its best to ensure its complete destruction. While a squad of us who had come together at a point in the road about four hundred yards from the bridge were shooting at such of these Federals as came in view, General Jackson, alone and unattended, rode up to us and suggested that we raise our sights, the enemy being at a greater distance from us than we thought. Adopting the suggestion, we fired a couple of volleys and then advanced with a rush to the bridge, the Federals taking flight before us. The flooring of the old bridge had burned away, but the stringers were not yet seriously damaged; and on these our squad crossed the stream and thence, unopposed, went on to the crest of the hill beyond.*
>
> *When the Texas Brigade, which was leading the advance of Jackson's command that day, overtook us, we moved steadily on, meeting no*

opposition, and just before dark reached Hundley's corner, in McClellan's rear. Here before midnight we were joined by the other troops then under Jackson's command.

Jackson sent some of his skirmishers across the creek, and Captain James Reilly from Rowan's North Carolina Artillery opened fire on the woods south of the Totopotomoy. During the shelling, Polegreen Church took its first cannon ball of the war—not to be its last. Thomas Williamson Hooper, a native of Hanover County who had grown up in Polegreen Church and was at the time of the war its pastor, reported that the church was struck by a shot from Jackson's flanking army.

The Texas–Georgia–South Carolina Brigade, supported by the North Carolina artillery, was followed by the First Maryland Infantry under Colonel Bradley T. Johnson, across the Totopotomoy, up the hill and on the road by Polegreen. Johnson reported as follows:

On Thursday, June 26, when the army advanced from Ashland the First Maryland Regiment, of my command, was ordered to the front by Major General Richard S. Ewell, with directions to drive in the enemy's pickets when found. In the afternoon Captain Nicholas, Company G, whom I had sent in advance skirmishing, discovered a cavalry picket at a church at the intersection of Hundley's Corner and Mechanicsville road. He immediately drove them in, and upon their receiving re-enforcements and making a stand I took Companies A and D and drove them over Beaver Creek. [The church mentioned in this report can be none other than Polegreen. Beaver Creek is undoubtedly Beaverdam Creek, whose headwaters at this point are a mile beyond Polegreen toward Mechanicsville.]

Jackson's engineers repaired the bridge over the Totopotomoy, and his weary troops trudged by Polegreen. Three-tenths of a mile south of the church is Hundley's Corner, where the road from Hanover Courthouse intersects the Shady Grove Church Road. Here, the head of Jackson's column halted and set up camp for the night.

From the bridge at the Totopotomoy southward through the open field across from Polegreen, which extends on down to Hundley's Corner, the twenty thousand troops of Jackson and Stuart were in bivouac while the Battle of Beaverdam Creek, a mile east of Mechanicsville, raged. Some of the unanswered and perplexing questions of the Civil War were in the making: Why was Jackson late? Why did A.P. Hill start the fight without Jackson? With three hours of daylight, why did Jackson not attack Porter's right and "roll it up" in the classic mode? Why were communications so bad between Lee's lieutenants? These and other questions related to Jackson's overnight camp across from Polegreen have been debated ever since June 26, 1862—the day Polegreen Church entered the war and the war entered Polegreen.

Before dawn on June 27, some of Jackson's forces began to stir and prepare for the continuation to their day's destination at Cold Harbor. Jackson understood he was to pass to the left of the head of Beaverdam Creek and be the flanking wing of the attacking forces. Stuart's cavalry was to be on Jackson's left, protecting the infantry and being Jackson's eyes. As the hours passed, the fields across from Polegreen and Hundley's Corner were emptied of their overnight guests, who went on to be participants in the Confederate victory at Gaines's Mill, the third day of combat in the Seven Days Battles. Polegreen Church was left to its quiet repose with an artillery shell in its side but otherwise undamaged. For almost two more years, the church continued to be what it had been designed and built to be—a place of worship. It stood as a continuing reminder of its earlier greatness as the house that Davies built.

Chapter 3

1864

No effort will be made here to detail or even outline the shifting fortunes of the war during the balance of 1862, 1863 and the first four months of 1864. It must be recalled, however, that during this nearly two-year period, furious engagements had occurred with incredible losses on both sides. Beginning with McClellan, Lee had defeated a series of commanders of the Army of the Potomac, whose chief mission was to defend Washington and enter Richmond. The terrible cost to both armies was to be remembered by names like Gaines's Mill, Cold Harbor, Malvern Hill, Antietam, Fredericksburg, Chancellorsville and Gettysburg.

The hope in the South was that the North would abandon, or at least compromise, its position on the subjugation of the South. This was not to be. The loss of life on both sides was horrible. The loss of property, of course, was mostly in the South. Because of its proximity to Washington, a disproportionate amount of the fighting and the damage that accompanied it occurred in Virginia. What the North could do, possessing a population nearly three times that of the South, was to provide almost endless replacements to cover its losses. There were times, however, when the war's high casualties caused sentiments in the North to turn toward cessation of the fighting. The last year of the war saw the armies of the Confederacy fighting more on heart than anything else. During that year, the Confederate forces rarely entered a battle in Virginia with odds better than two to one in favor of the Federals. So it was as the battles along the Totopotomoy began to unfold in late May 1864.

The winter of 1863–64 had been a cold and stormy one. In spite of all efforts, there was a limit to what could be done to feed the Confederate army during those long months. A deteriorating rail transportation system added to the difficulty. Many a soldier's letter home or personal diary records the experience of hunger rarely satisfied. In camp, on the march or called into battle on an empty stomach, few sufferings short of death or serious injury compared to that of little or no rations to eat. Willy Dame, as he was known by his comrades during the war, was an Episcopal clergyman for fifty years. After the conflict ended, he left an account of what food rations were like the winter before the Totopotomoy battles:

> *The one thing that we suffered most from, the hardship hardest to bear was hunger. The scantiness of the rations was something fierce. We never got a square meal that winter. We were always hungry. Even when we were getting full rations the issue was one-quarter pound of bacon, or one-half pound of beef and little over a pint of flour or cornmeal, ground with the cob on it, we used to think—no stated ration of vegetables or sugar and coffee—just bread and meat. Some days we had the bread, but no meat; some days the meat, but no bread. Two days we had nothing, neither bread nor meat—and it was a solemn and empty crowd. Now and then, at long intervals, they gave us some dried peas. Occasionally, a little sugar—about an ounce to a man for a three days' [sic] ration. The Orderly of the mess would spread the whole amount on the back of a tin plate, and mark off thirteen portions, and put each man's share into his hand—three days' rations, this was.*

Across the Blue Ridge, the breadbasket of the Army of Northern Virginia, the Shenandoah Valley, beginning in late May 1864, was systematically pillaged. On many a farm, what had not been destroyed by invaders was burned. Civilian populations, particularly in places such as Richmond, shared the suffering of the army in the field. In early April, there were riots in the streets of the Confederate capital. Women were crying out, "Give us bread or peace."

The Civil War, like many events in human history marked by suffering and deprivation, produced its share of examples of mankind's effort to triumph over adversity with a touch of humor. Coincidental with Robert E. Lee's assumption of the command of the Army of Northern Virginia in 1862, Victor Hugo's *Les Misérables* was published and widely read. It didn't take long for Lee's army to proudly refer to itself in its inadequately provided for soldierly state as "Lee's Miserables."

In early March, President Abraham Lincoln had placed Ulysses S. Grant in command of the Union armies. Grant chose to accompany the Army of the Potomac. It was Lincoln's and Grant's common conviction that the knockout blow for the Confederacy would be the defeat of Lee and the capture of Richmond. To this end, all possible preparations were made. An analysis of the strength in numbers, equipment, resources of food, clothing, munitions and available artillery and cavalry horses of the two opposing armies can be viewed only as near invincible odds against which the Army of Northern Virginia fought yet another campaign.

Yet an indomitable trust in Lee had developed since June 1, 1862, making Lee's "boys" believe it would take greater odds than that to defeat them. The civilian population of the Confederate capital in Richmond likewise viewed the coming of the freshly uniformed Federals under a new commander as little cause for alarm. While discouraging news had been coming to Richmond from the west and Deep South for months, the forces under Lee in Virginia still believed that victory was possible in this sector of the Confederacy. And if, with a little luck or providential intervention, Lee could hit Grant at the right time and place with an offensive and crush him, the Federal government might entertain an armistice.

While Lee's strategy had the appearance of being a continual defensive maneuver during this "last campaign" in 1864, he did not abandon the idea of an offensive thrust employing the deceased Jackson's famous flanking moves. During the long campaign from the Wilderness to the beginning of the Siege of Petersburg, there were several times when Lee felt this was possible. At North Anna, Lee came close to drawing the Army of the Potomac into a trap that could have been serious, if not disastrous, for Grant.

As the days continued to lengthen and warm in April 1864, the realization that the Army of Northern Virginia, from a purely physical standpoint, faced a herculean task even to survive surfaced. Men and horses had eaten barely enough through the winter to stay alive. Grant's delay in opening up the spring campaign was greeted favorably in that the horses could get some forage from new grasses. The morale of Lee's army under these circumstances was amazingly high. It could be accounted for in terms of the men's confidence in their commander and in the justice of their cause—that cause being the defense of their homeland in a resistance to tyranny similar to what most Confederates, particularly Virginians, believed was in the spirit of 1776. Lee's role as leader of the Army of Northern Virginia was not only that of military commander but also that of its spiritual force. A week before the expected launching of Grant's offensive, Lee wrote to his son "Rooney," "Our country demands all our strength, all our energies. To resist the powerful combination now forming against us will require every man in his place. If victorious, we have everything to hope for in the future. If defeated, nothing will be left for us to live for…My whole trust is in God, and I am ready for whatever he may ordain." This trust in God, which was to sustain him during the bitterest time of his life—his surrender at Appomattox Court House—was embodied in him as he looked out on the Union army on the morning of May 2 from the Confederate observation post on Clark Mountain. Below him in the fields around Culpeper was a vast array of military power—well fed and well equipped.

The following day, May 3, would be the last quiet day for the next six weeks. During the day, orders were given within the Army of the Potomac to prepare to move out during the night. On the morning of May 4, the fields around Culpeper were empty, and the Union army could be seen marching to the southeast. Lee could not be certain exactly what the new Union commander, Grant, had in mind, but he was confident it involved some attempt to turn his right. With a force of 61,000 men, Lee began to deploy his troops to contest the maneuver of Grant, who commanded 120,000. He ordered A.P. Hill to advance on the plank road and Richard S. Ewell on the Orange Turnpike, which paralleled Grant's movement taking place still north of the Rapidan. Lee himself rode along with Hill at the head of his troops and bivouacked the night of the fourth at Verdiersville.

The Confederate commander, faced with an opponent who possessed men and ordnance in superior strength, was constantly forced to employ any other advantage that presented itself or could be developed. In the first day of this campaign, Lee awaited news of Grant's intended line of march. If Richmond was the objective, at some point, the Union army would be compelled to cross the Rapidan. It was Lee's hope that Grant would do this soon and be forced to contend with the disadvantages of fighting in the Wilderness, a tangle of trees and underbrush, hampering both infantry and artillery movement.

By 2:00 p.m. on May 5, the main body of the Union army was in the Wilderness, with fighting breaking out at several points. Firing was heavy, as were the casualties, between Ewell's and Hill's corps and three corps of the enemy until after dark. The Confederates had at least contained the Union forces in their first encounter.

May 6 was a day to be remembered by all who were within sight of the commander of the Army of Northern Virginia. Longstreet had been slow to arrive and take his position on the field in support of Hill. The Federal infantry was attacking Hill with strength and determination. The Union attack began at 5:00 a.m., and shortly thereafter, Hill's line began to crumble. Lee had every reason to feel a sense of desperation as he watched Cadmus M. Wilcox's men returning from the front, offering no resistance. Where, under heaven, was Longstreet? When it seemed that Hill's artillery was about to be overrun, Lee stepped up and ordered the artillery commander, Colonel William Pogue, to open fire. Several rounds momentarily slowed down the Union advance. Just at that moment, the first of Longstreet's corps arrived—Hood's Texans now led by John Gregg. Upon seeing these ragged but determined men, Lee inquired loudly as to their identity. In answering, the increasing number cried out, "Texas boys!"

Lee's emotion took over, and composure aside, he shouted, "Hurrah for Texas, hurrah for Texas!" But it didn't stop there. The commander of the Army of Northern Virginia, on Traveller, dashed along the forming line, shaping it into a force for a counter charge. Then he made a move that alarmed his men. He reined Traveller to the right and headed directly toward the enemy on the heels of the Texan Arkansans.

When the startled infantry saw what he proposed to do and the risk at hand, they cried out, "Go back, General Lee, go back! We won't go on unless you go back!" General Gregg and a sergeant tried to stop him, without success. Only when his aide Colonel Venable dashed up and called out that he needed to give Longstreet his orders did Lee turn around, averting what could have been an unparalleled disaster.

The second incident of the day did not have such a satisfactory ending. By 10:00 a.m., the fighting had subsided, but within an hour, the Confederates opened up an attack on the left of the Federals, which met with such success that Longstreet believed he could roll up the enemy's lines and drive them back to the Rapidan. At the peak of this optimism, the jungle of the Wilderness and the disorderliness of the Confederate lines resulted in the incredible occurring. In the same Wilderness where Jackson had fallen a year before, the victim of friendly fire, Longstreet now became a casualty of the same. He was painfully wounded, and the Spring Campaign for him was finished.

The firing ended on the sixth at dusk, with heavy casualties on both sides, but heavier for the Union army. The night itself was a horror. Many who had not been killed outright were trapped in the smoke and flames of trees and low brush ignited by the artillery. The screams of the wounded unable to crawl to safety were remembered by both armies long after the war had ended.

On the seventh, neither army attacked. Instead, Grant decided to extricate himself from the Wilderness and move off to the southeast. In 1863, General Joseph Hooker, on the heels of his defeat in this same Wilderness, had withdrawn the Army of the Potomac to the north side of the Rappahannock, but Lee expected that Grant would do otherwise and keep up the pressure on the road to Richmond. With what some of his lieutenants perceived as an uncanny ability to anticipate the action of the enemy, Lee believed that Grant would move next to Spotsylvania. The Southern commander reasoned that the opposing army commanders would do what they should do in a particular situation. Therefore, placing himself in Grant's shoes, with Richmond as the objective, he would strike for the critical railroad junction where the Central Virginia and the Richmond, Fredericksburg & Potomac Railroads crossed one another. The shortest route to Hanover Junction was through Spotsylvania Courthouse.

As the day wore on, the intelligence from the front regarding Grant's troop movements confirmed Lee's expectation. Following the wounding of Longstreet, General "Dick" Anderson was placed in temporary command of the First Corps, with orders to move to Spotsylvania as soon after dark as possible, the men having been withdrawn from the line and given some time to rest. As it turned out, Anderson did move his men out of the earthworks after dark, but the woods being on fire in every direction, there was no safe place for his men to rest. He felt compelled to keep his troops on the move over a narrow and frequently obstructed road and get as close to Spotsylvania Courthouse as possible before daybreak on the eighth. It proved to be a blessing in disguise, for it put the Confederate soldiers near the courthouse just before Grant's vanguard arrived.

No time was lost in Anderson's corps having to defend its early arrival at Spotsylvania Courthouse. The forces of Ewell and Jubal A. Early, who had replaced the ill Hill, soon joined Anderson and were positioned to defend Laurel Hill. Earthworks were erected by the Confederates roughly in the shape of an inverted V, which was dubbed the "Mule-Shoe." For three days, heavy offensive sparring by Union forces was fought off by the Confederates, but at 6:00 p.m. on May 10, the small attacks were followed by a heavy artillery bombardment, followed by concentrated infantry assault that broke the Confederate line. The Southern troops were rallied and recovered lost ground. There were heavy casualties on both sides, yet they were heavier on the Union.

In the predawn of the twelfth, at 4:30 a.m., the Federals opened up another assault. Again the Confederate defense was penetrated, this time at the angle. Lee was at the front on Traveller, giving orders and rallying the dislodged Confederate infantry. Again in the midst of a desperate situation, he was caught up in the spirit of the moment, and raising his hat, he reined Traveller into the face of the enemy. Douglas S. Freeman described the moment vividly as follows:

> *By this time a searching fire was penetrating the woods where the gray coats were taking position. General John B. Gordon himself had just escaped death from a bullet that grazed his coat, not an inch from his spine, but when he saw Lee's position, he realized that the General was preparing to join in the charge and he broke out dramatically, "General Lee, this is no place for you. Go back, General; we will drive them back. These men are Virginians and Georgians. They have never failed. They never will. Will you, boys?"*
>
> *"No, no," cried every man within hearing distance.*
>
> *"General Lee to the rear; Lee to the rear!"*
>
> *"Go back, General Lee, we can't charge until you go back!"*
>
> *"We will drive them back, General!"*
>
> *Gordon and some of his officers placed their mounts between him and the enemy, whose fire had come nearer and had increased ominously during the few seconds of delay. A minute more and the enemy would be upon them. Gordon did not wait on military etiquette. Leaning forward, he caught hold of Traveller's bridle, but in the crowding of the flanks of the two brigades, which were now ready to advance, Gordon was pushed behind Lee. Thereupon a sergeant of the Forty-ninth Virginia seized Traveller by the reins and jerked his head to the rear.*
>
> *As Lee rode unwillingly back a few paces, he heard the clear voice of Gordon above the roar of the musketry: "Forward! Guide right!"*

In less than an hour, along another sector of the line where General Nathaniel Harris's Mississippians were being assaulted, Lee again was in the thick of the fighting and again was forced by his own troops to go to the rear.

By noon, the Confederates had forced the Union troops back over the angular parapet at the Mule Shoe. On this day, the combatants were to give it a new name, "Bloody Angle." The assaults by the Union troops were continuous and fierce, only to be matched by the determination of the Confederates. Much of the combat was hand to hand. The losses were staggering. Fighting went on for sixteen hours with no letup, most getting no food and none getting any rest. "In all the bloody story of that mad, criminal war there had not been such a hideous ordeal," wrote Freeman.

The fighting of the twelfth flowed into the thirteenth. During the darkness, the Confederates were withdrawn to a secondary line behind the parapet. They left countless dead in the trenches behind the parapet and more piled up just behind the trench, placed there by their comrades after having been killed. In the midst of the battle, the Confederate commander had received a messenger from Richmond with the worst kind of news. General J.E.B. Stuart, who had been sent off to interrupt General Philip Sheridan's cavalry, which had done great damage to the Confederate supply trains at Beaverdam Station and was headed for Richmond, had been mortally wounded on the afternoon of the eleventh. When Lee received a second message on the thirteenth, he learned that Stuart had died in Richmond at 8:00 p.m. on the twelfth. The revered commander of the Army of Northern Virginia could not conceal his grief and sense of personal loss. Stuart was dead at thirty-one years old. It was not possible to replace him. At the first news of the wounding, Lee said to his staff surrounding him, "He never brought me a piece of false information."

The rain that had contributed to the discomfort and ability to fight on the twelfth continued for the next five days and caused military operations to be discontinued. For the survivors of the awful conflict at the Bloody Angle, it seemed a godsend. Except for another general assault on Lee's new line south of the Harrison House on May 18, which was easily repulsed, no other major attacks were launched by Grant at Spotsylvania. While Lee expected Grant to make another move to the south, he could not be certain what the Union commander had in mind. An abortive effort by Ewell to determine if Grant's left wing had moved off resulted in no more than confirmation that it had not, though it cost Ewell about nine hundred casualties in dead, wounded and missing to learn this. Finally, on the morning of May 21, Lee learned that Union forces were headed toward Milford and Hanover Junction. Lee reacted to this move by Grant by ordering his army to the south bank of the North Anna. The position was perilously close to the Confederate capital, but it offered the best possibilities for the city's defense, as other alternatives presented easier ways for Grant to pin Lee down while sending in forces from the flank that might get between Lee and Richmond.

Though Grant had the advantage of a head start, Lee was able to overcome it and arrived at the North Anna and Hanover Junction. By the morning of the twenty-second, the Second Corps (Ewell) was arriving, closely followed by the First (Anderson), with the Third (Hill) not far behind. Lee did not order destruction of the bridges over the North Anna because he calculated that Grant might not choose to fight his way straight through to Hanover

Junction but rather move off on the north side of the river to engage the Confederates at some other place. Should Lee wish to attack Grant in such a case, he would need the bridges for recrossing.

By noon on the twenty-third, great numbers of Union men were observed on the north bank of the North Anna. Warren's corps (Fifth) crossed over the river at Jerricho Mill at 3:00 p.m. and, meeting poorly organized resistance, established Grant's right wing south of the North Anna. Four hours later, the Union army overwhelmed a small Confederate garrison at Chesterfield Bridge on Grant's left wing and poured across the North Anna as dark settled over the eight-mile-long front. The situation might have appeared grim to most commanders, but Lee saw the opportunity that was present in it.

Even though he was in the early stages of an intestinal malady that was to distress him for ten days, so much so that he could not ride Traveller, Lee's mind was at this stage prepared for the challenge. He ordered Hill to pull back to the southeast about four miles and take up a line perpendicular across the Central Virginia Railroad. He ordered Anderson to a position in the center near Ox Ford. High bluffs guarded the south bank at this point, running along the river for a mile. Ewell was ordered also to pull back from the river, connect with Anderson's right and cover the front down to Hanover Junction. In so doing, Lee reduced the distance between his right wing and his left by 50 percent, eased his communication problem and increased his ability to move troops from one wing to another if support were needed. The defense line of the Confederates appeared as a wedge in the center of the Union line, a wide inverted V. If Grant wished to reinforce either wing of the Army of the Potomac, he would be forced to cross the river twice. A Federal attack by Ambrose Burnside's corps was ordered in the center, but Anderson's men easily repulsed it.

On the twenty-fifth, Lee felt worse but still attempted to carry out his work. As in similar situations when there was an expectation of remaining in position for more than a few hours, each army proceeded to dig in. Any opportunity that Lee had hoped for in striking an offensive blow had rapidly diminished by late on the twenty-fourth, and Grant by this time also concluded that an assault on his part would be too costly. Heavy demonstrations by the Union army took place all day on the twenty-sixth, designed to give the appearance that Grant might make his move toward Richmond by moving around Lee's left. Any uncertainty that Lee may have felt was resolved when the Confederates awakened on the twenty-seventh. On their front, the enemy had disappeared. Grant had ordered both wings of his army back to the north bank of the river and was marching them to the southeast, beyond the confluence of the North and South Anna Rivers, which, from that point on to West Point, bears the name Pamunkey.

It is sometimes assumed that Grant's strategy upon launching his offensive across the Rapidan was to avoid a frontal attack on the Army of Northern Virginia and to outflank Lee by moving around the Confederates' right, getting the Army of the Potomac between Lee and Richmond. This theory doesn't hold up in light of several factors. Grant seemed to be testing the possibilities of frontal attack on a number of occasions, only to back off and shift to his left. Brigadier General John Gibbon, division commander in Major General Winfield Scott Hancock's Second Corps, wrote, "From the 14th to the 19th, the time was taken up in various movements, both to the left and back to the right, with efforts to find some weak point in the enemy's line where we could assault with some prospect of success." Another factor that undoubtedly determined Grant's use of his forces is reflected in Gibbon's summary of the 1864 campaign through the first month of battle:

Two things up to this time [May 31] *had been well demonstrated. We had never succeeded in forcing Lee, by battle, from any position he assumed, nor had he succeeded in forcing us from any. Twice we had succeeded in effecting a lodgment in his line, but in neither case was the position of his army essentially affected. A few hours were all that was necessary to render any position so strong by breastworks that the opposite party was unable to carry it, and it became a recognized fact amongst the men themselves that when the enemy had occupied a position six or eight hours ahead of us, it was useless to attempt to take it. This feeling became so marked that, when troops under these circumstances were ordered forward, they went a certain distance and then lay down and opened fire. It became a saying in the army that when the old troops got as far forward as they thought they ought to go, "they sat down and made coffee."*

Chapter 4

Who Were They at the Totopotomoy in '64?

During the first five days after the Pamunkey crossing by the Army of the Potomac on May 26, 1864, the combined forces of that army and the Army of Northern Virginia of the Confederacy numbered at least 175,000 men. Many of the men in gray had been in Hanover County two years before during the Seven Days Battles. Some of these men were born there and had walked or ridden horses in peaceful pursuits on the roads on which they now marched. Besides Virginians, other Southerners came from the Carolinas, Louisiana, Georgia, Maryland, Alabama, Mississippi, Florida, Tennessee, Texas and Arkansas.

The men in blue were from Pennsylvania, New Jersey, New York, Michigan, Wisconsin, Maryland, Massachusetts, Maine, Connecticut, Delaware, Indiana, Ohio, West Virginia, Vermont, Rhode Island, New Hampshire, Minnesota and Illinois.

War has always been more, much more, than troop strength, armaments, supplies, food, medicine and all those material and physical factors that are commonly associated with military conflict. At the most fundamental level, war is men destroying one another. The element of this war that made it so different from any in which this country has engaged before or since was that the men destroying one another were brothers and former friends. What was taking place at the Battle of Polegreen Church is an example of this dreadful phenomenon.

The purpose of this present digression in the narrative of the battle of Polegreen is to focus attention, all too briefly, on some of the key figures in the drama unfolding in Hanover County in 1864. The well-known actors, such as Lee, Grant and Meade; the lesser-known participants, such as the corps commanders—Hancock, Burnside, Warren and Wright for the Union and A.P. Hill, Anderson and Early for the Confederacy; the almost-unknown division commanders John Gibbon (U.S.) and Henry Heth (CSA); and enlisted men James Aubery (U.S.) and William S. White (CSA) all played a part at Polegreen in the hostilities that took place between May 28 and June 3, 1864.

These brief glimpses of the men named above cannot be called biographical sketches. Rather, they give some indication of who they were; how, in some cases, their paths had crossed prior to the war; and what made this particular war so different from most. While little is written here pertaining to the lives of these men after the war, the reader will find the lives of most who survived the conflict to be exceedingly interesting during the years following Appomattox Court House.

GENERALS

Robert E. Lee

Robert E. Lee was the son of a hero of the Revolutionary War, "Light Horse Harry" Lee, and Ann Hill Carter. He was born in Westmoreland County, Virginia, in January 1807. His father's ill-advised land investments and poor management of finances forced Robert and his mother out of the homestead at Stratford Hall and caused significant hardship for the family, who were compelled to live in modest circumstances in Alexandria. Lee received an appointment to West Point in the class of 1829 and graduated second in his class. During his four years at the military academy, he did not receive a single demerit against his name. He was commissioned a second lieutenant in the Corps of Engineers, and for the next seventeen years, he carried out his duties in a number of military posts. He was the engineer in charge of the design and improvement of St. Louis Harbor. When the war with Mexico exploded in 1846, he won the praise and confidence of Major General Winfield Scott and emerged from the conflict with a brevet rank of colonel. Lee was appointed superintendent of West Point in 1852. Three years later, he was commissioned lieutenant colonel and was sent to Texas, where he pulled duty until the outbreak of the Civil War.

A portrait of General Robert E. Lee, officer of the Confederate army. *Courtesy of the Library of Congress.*

The hysteria for war, fanned largely by politicians in the North and South, had within three days—from April 12 to 15, 1861—erupted into the bombardment of Fort Sumter and Lincoln's proclamation calling for seventy-five thousand troops to suppress the rebellion. Not a soldier, Northern or Southern, had been killed during the Sumter bombardment. Yet it was no longer possible for passions to be controlled by reason, and Virginia knew it was to be invaded. Lee was called to Washington by his friend, General in Chief Winfield Scott, and through intermediary Francis P. Blair, Lincoln's offer to Lee of the leadership of the U.S. Army assembling in and around Washington was made. Lee, the descendant of founders of the Virginia Colony and a Revolutionary War hero, could not raise his sword against his homeland. On April 18, he told Scott of his interview with Blair: "I declined the offer he made me to take command of the army that was to be brought into the field, stating as cordially and as courteously as I could, that though opposed to secession and deprecating war, I could take no part in an invasion of the Southern States." Lee personally owned no slaves, but as executor for his father-in-law's estate, he inherited the task of manumitting the slaves for which he became responsible. Here on the south side of the Totopotomoy in Hanover County, Lee was living out his premonition of what was going to happen in the United States he had served faithfully for thirty-three years. There is an interesting phenomenon relating to Lee that speaks much of his attitude toward the North during the war years. When he chose to make reference to the Northern army, he most often simply did so by referring to "those people" rather than "the enemy."

Ulysses S. Grant

On the north side of the Totopotomoy, the commander of all Northern forces was a soldier who had fought in that same Mexican War, U.S. Grant. The leaders of the two armies were former comrades turned enemies.

Ulysses Simpson Grant was born in Point Pleasant, Ohio, in 1822 and received his appointment to West Point in 1839. He was an average student academically but far above average as a horseman. Since there were no vacancies in the U.S. cavalry regiments at the time of Grant's graduation, he was given the rank of second lieutenant of infantry. During the war in Mexico, he distinguished himself on several occasions and emerged with the brevet rank of captain. He resigned from the army in 1854, following admonishment from his commanding officer concerning his drinking

General U.S. Grant, three-quarter-length portrait, in uniform. *Courtesy of the Library of Congress.*

and gambling. As a civilian, his life was mediocre or less, and even in the early months of the Civil War, he was virtually ignored by Major General George B. McClellan, then in Ohio, and the adjutant general in Washington following his application for duty. Grant had a connection with an influential member of the Illinois congressional delegation, who obtained for him the rank of brigadier general. He enjoyed a series of successes, despite one near disaster, in Tennessee and Mississippi and had gained the attention of the nation by 1863, at which time he received appointment as major general in the regular army.

By early 1864, Grant was promoted to lieutenant general and given command of all the Union armies. He developed a plan to defeat the Southern forces on three fronts. General Meade and the Army of the Potomac began their attack on Richmond from the north, Major General Benjamin F. Butler and the Army of the James pressured Richmond from the south and Major General William T. Sherman and the armies of the Ohio, Tennessee and Cumberland thrust deep into northwest Georgia with the dual mission of defeating the Confederate Army of Tennessee and capturing Atlanta. Grant made his headquarters with Meade, thus for all practical purpose putting him in field command opposite General Lee. Grant demanded and obtained from the Federal government virtually unlimited resources of men and material and, at times, used them with abandon, such as at Cold Harbor, when on June 3 he suffered four to five thousand killed and wounded, many in less than an hour, in repeated assaults on well-entrenched but numerically inferior Confederate troops. One account erroneously reported that the casualties and wounded occurred in less than eight minutes. One fact is certain: Grant lost more men from the Rapidan to Petersburg than Lee had in his army at the opening of the campaign. The Union war of attrition finally paid off. After the Siege of Petersburg, which lasted ten months, Lee was compelled to evacuate and, seven days later, surrendered at Appomattox Court House.

In concentrating attention on that phase of the campaign of 1864 that immediately preceded the Battle of Cold Harbor and which occurred on the northern flank of the two armies in the vicinity of the Totopotomoy and Polegreen Church, we will take particular note of both armies' corps' and divisions' leadership between May 26 and June 1. Four Federal corps were actively fighting in the Army of the Potomac during this period. On the Confederate side, there were three corps plus two brigades borrowed from the Shenandoah Valley. Grant's four corps commanders were Winfield Scott Hancock, Second Corps; Ambrose Everett Burnside, Ninth Corps; Horatio Gouverneur Wright, Sixth Corps; and Gouverneur K. Warren, Fifth Corps. Lee's three corps commanders were Richard Heron Anderson, First Corps (Longstreet's corp, as he had been wounded in the Battle of the Wilderness); Jubal Anderson Early, Second Corps (Ewell's corp, as he was ill with diarrhea); Ambrose Powell Hill, Third Corps; and John Cabell Breckinridge's valley command.

George Meade

A portrait of Major General George G. Meade, officer in the Federal army. *Courtesy of the Library of Congress.*

George Gordon Meade's father was an American merchant in Spain who was financially ruined from choosing the wrong allegiance during the Napoleonic Wars. George was born there in 1815. He graduated from West Point in 1835 and quit the army a year later to become a civil engineer. Six years later, he rejoined and became a second lieutenant in the Corps of Topographical Engineers. He, too, served with the U.S. Army in the Mexican War. Like many other West Point graduates, he was made a brigadier general of volunteers shortly after the Civil War began. He was given command of one of the three brigades of the Pennsylvania Reserves in the division of Brigadier General George McCall, who joined General George B. McClellan on the Middle Peninsula in mid-June 1862 and was severely wounded in the Seven Days Battles. The following year, on June 28, he was placed in command of the Army of the Potomac, just in time to command at Gettysburg. Having repulsed the repeated Confederate assaults, Meade's hesitation in following up and routing the badly mauled troops of Lee brought much criticism on him from President Lincoln. The administration backed down when it became apparent that the general public was pleased with the Federal success at Gettysburg. In the early spring of 1864, when Grant was made general in chief of the Federal armies, the new commander chose to make his field headquarters with the Army of the Potomac. The Federal high command during the last year of the war was a strange configuration. Nominally in command of the Army of the Potomac,

Meade nevertheless took orders from Grant until the end of the war. At the same time, corps commander Burnside outranked Meade by seniority, yet Meade was his commander. To accommodate the situation, Burnside took his orders directly from Grant until the fourth week of May. Meade died in Philadelphia seven years after Appomattox.

Winfield S. Hancock

Winfield S. Hancock grew up in Norristown, Pennsylvania, eleven miles from his birthplace in Montgomery Square. He graduated from West Point in 1844, earned a brevet for gallantry in the Mexican War and was engaged against the Seminole Indians and in the U.S. effort to keep the Mormons in line. Several months after the Civil War was underway, on September 23, 1861, he was made a brigadier general of volunteers in McClellan's Army of the Potomac. He fought at Williamsburg, Seven Days, Antietam, Fredericksburg and Chancellorsville. He distinguished himself at Gettysburg, where he was wounded when a bullet drove bits of wood and a nail from his saddle into his groin and disabled him for six months. Hancock's corps saw heavy action all the way from the Rapidan to Petersburg in the spring and summer of 1864. His corps did most of the Federal fighting on the right flank of the Army of the Potomac from May 29 to June 1 and was to suffer heavy casualties at Cold Harbor on June 3.

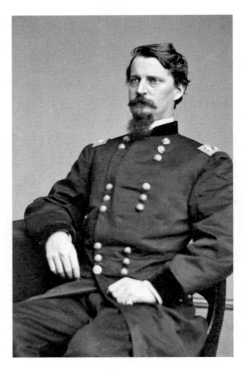

A portrait of Major General Winfield S. Hancock, officer in the Federal army. *Courtesy of the Library of Congress.*

Ambrose E. Burnside

General Ambrose E. Burnside, head-and-shoulders portrait, in military uniform. *Courtesy of the Library of Congress.*

Ambrose Everett Burnside was born in Liberty, Indiana, son of a South Carolinian who had been a slave owner but had freed his slaves when he moved north. Burnside graduated from West Point in 1847 and went to Mexico, but he saw little action, as he was on garrison duty in Mexico City. He resigned his commission, left the army in 1853 and worked later for his friend George B. McClellan on the Illinois Central Railroad. When the Civil War began, he organized a volunteer brigade in Rhode Island, went to Washington and fought at First Manassas. When the reluctant McClellan was finally relieved of his command of the Army of the Potomac, following the failure of the Peninsula Campaign and his failure to aggressively follow up on his victory at Antietam, Burnside was given his command. However, a month later, his failure to dislodge Lee's army at Fredericksburg, where the Union army suffered almost more than thirteen thousand casualties, cost him his job as commander. Burnside had sought to relieve Major General Joseph Hooker and several other senior Army of the Potomac generals for disloyalty and insubordination following the Fredericksburg debacle and the "Mud March." Instead, Lincoln put Hooker in command of the Army of the Potomac in place of Burnside. The Ninth Corps, after service in the west, was recruited up to full strength in the spring of 1864, and Burnside rejoined the Army of the Potomac, this time under George Meade, whom he outranked. His command did not distinguish itself at any time, from the crossing of the Rapidan until the Battle of the Crater on July 30. Burnside was relieved as commander of the Ninth Corps in mid-August, some two weeks after the Crater debacle.

Gouverneur K. Warren

Gouverneur Kimble Warren was a native of New York, having been born in Cold Spring across the Hudson River in view of West Point. He saw the light of day on January 8, 1830, and, at age sixteen, received an appointment to the Military Academy, graduating when he was twenty years old, ranking second in the class of 1850. He made the military his career, serving initially as a topographical engineer and then as instructor in mathematics at West Point. Shortly after the outbreak of hostilities in the Civil War, he was appointed a lieutenant colonel of the Fifth New York. On June 27, 1862, he was wounded in the Seven Days Battles at Gaines's Mill. At that time, Fitz John Porter was commander of the Fifth Corps, and Warren, now a colonel, was a brigade commander in George Sykes's division of that corps. Warren maintained the command of his brigade in the Battles of Second Manassas and Antietam. He was promoted to brigadier general of volunteers.

By the time the two armies faced each other at Gettysburg, Warren was the chief engineer of the Army of the Potomac. Though he did not command troops on the battle line, he is credited with exemplary perception and action in dashing toward a weak spot in the Union line at Little Round Top, which

was threatened by attacking Confederates. There he rallied two brigades of Sykes's Fifth Corps to hold that strategic feature and prevent Meade's left flank from being rolled up, assuring the Army of the Potomac success on the second day at Gettysburg. When Hancock was wounded at Gettysburg, Warren was put in temporary command of the Second Corps.

A portrait of Major General Gouverneur K. Warren, officer in the Federal army. *Courtesy of the Library of Congress.*

In the spring of 1864, Warren was placed in command of the Fifth Corps and served in Grant's Overland Campaign from the Rapidan to Petersburg. Philip Sheridan is credited with undermining General Grant's confidence in Warren, and when Sheridan was given authority to relieve Warren of his command, he did so without hesitation or propriety. Sheridan's reason for removing Warren was his handling of his command in the Battle of Five Forks. Fourteen years after the war ended, a court of inquiry upheld Warren and criticized the way he was relieved from his duties, which had ruined his military career. Warren's Fifth Corps was the first to cross the Totopotomoy Creek during the several days of fighting that occurred along that stream. He died on August 8, 1882, at his home in Newport, Rhode Island.

Horatio G. Wright

Horatio Gouverneur Wright, a native of Connecticut, was appointed to West Point, from where he graduated second in the class of 1841. He served in the Corps of Engineers until the beginning of the Civil War. Early in the war, on April 20, 1861, the Federals attempted to destroy the Norfolk Navy Yard, and Wright was assigned to the operation. The effort failed, and he was taken prisoner by Virginia troops. Later, he was released in time to face the Confederate guns in the First Battle of Manassas, still serving as an engineer. In September, he was made a brigadier general of volunteers.

H.G. Wright. *Courtesy of the Library of Congress.*

His career was relatively uneventful throughout the war. He commanded a division of John Sedgwick's Sixth Corps at Gettysburg in 1863. In Grant's campaign in May 1864, he led his division into the Wilderness, and when Sedgwick was killed at Spotsylvania, Wright was elevated to the command of the Sixth Corps. Thus, Wright had been a corps commander only two weeks when he crossed the Pamunkey and held the right flank of the Army of the Potomac between the upper Totopotomoy and Hanover Courthouse. He seems not to have lived up to Grant's expectation at Cold Harbor. After the war, Wright remained in army service as chief engineer until his retirement in 1884.

Philip H. Sheridan

Major General P.H. Sheridan. *Courtesy of the Library of Congress.*

In his memoirs, Philip Henry Sheridan says he was born in Albany, New York, in 1831 but from infancy lived in Somerset, Ohio, until his appointment to West Point, resulting from another appointee's failure to surmount the entrance examination. He was in the class of 1852 but was suspended for a year for fighting with Cadet Sergeant William Terrell. Following graduation, he served on the western frontier until the outbreak of the Civil War. A number of his superiors resigned the service to join the Confederate forces, thereby opening the path for his promotion to chief quartermaster and commissary of the Army of Southwest Missouri. In May 1862, he was made colonel of the Second Michigan Cavalry, and like several of the Union corps and division commanders already mentioned, he was made brigadier general of volunteers in September 1862. In the late summer of 1862, Sheridan became an infantry division commander in the Army of the Ohio (redesignated the Army of the Cumberland in late October 1862). He led his division at Perryville, Stones River and Chickamauga and gained the attention of U.S. Grant by his success at Missionary Ridge on November 25, 1863. Grant placed him in charge of all the cavalry attached to the Army of the Potomac in the spring of 1864.

Sheridan managed to reap the benefits of a press that magnified his successes and glossed over the number of casualties that attended them. Sheridan's tactics of destroying everything remotely supporting the Confederate military effort in the Valley of Virginia, starting in October 1864, gained him contempt in the South comparable only to that of William T. Sherman.

CONFEDERATE COMMANDERS AT POLEGREEN

Richard H. Anderson (First Corps)

Richard Heron Anderson, a native of South Carolina, was born in Sumter County at "Hill Crest" in 1821. He was a member of the famous class of 1842 at West Point and was brevetted a first lieutenant in the Mexican War. He had become a captain by the outbreak of the Civil War and resigned his commission in March 1861 to join the Confederate service. He witnessed the bombardment of Fort Sumter and, in July, was promoted to brigadier general in command of Charleston when General P.G.T. Beauregard went to Virginia. Next, he served as a brigade commander at Pensacola under Major General Braxton Bragg. Anderson was assigned to Longstreet's division as a brigade commander during McClellan's Peninsula Campaign. He was promoted to major general on July 14, 1862, as a division commander in the First Corps. After Chancellorsville and Stonewall Jackson's death, he and his division were transferred into A.P. Hill's Third Corps. When Longstreet was wounded in the Battle of the Wilderness on May 6, 1864, he assumed the temporary command of the First Corps and was promoted to lieutenant general while in command in front of Polegreen on May 31, 1864.

Jubal A. Early (Second Corps)

Jubal Anderson Early was born in 1816 in Franklin County, Virginia, and gained appointment to West Point in 1833. He graduated in four years, spent one year fighting in Florida's Second Seminole War and

Confederate general Jubal Early. *Courtesy of the Library of Congress.*

left the army. Returning to Virginia, he studied law and entered politics, being elected to the House of Delegates and commonwealth's attorney. He reentered the army when the U.S. went to war against Mexico. Like many Virginians, in the service and outside, he opposed secession and voted against it in the Virginia convention of April 1861. When Lincoln mobilized an army to invade the South, he entered the Confederate army as a colonel and led a brigade that included the Twenty-fourth Virginia Infantry in the First Battle of Manassas. After Lee took over command of the Army of Northern Virginia, Early fought in every engagement except the Seven Days Battles for the next two years. When Ewell became ill at North Anna, Early was given his command and, like Anderson, was promoted to lieutenant general while in front of Polegreen on May 31, 1864.

Ambrose P. Hill (Third Corps)

General A.P. Hill, CSA. *Courtesy of Wikimedia Commons.*

Ambrose Powell Hill was born in Culpeper, Virginia, in 1825. He entered West Point in 1842 and matriculated in the star-studded class of 1846, but because of illness, he did not graduate until 1847. Like Early, he served during the Mexican War and fought in the Third Seminole War. Loyal to his state, he resigned from the U.S. Army and entered the Confederate service in March 1861. He was made brigadier general in February 1862, and as McClellan was coming up the Middle Peninsula toward Richmond, he acquitted himself admirably at Williamsburg and especially during the Seven Days Battles north of the Chickahominy. Following this Confederate repulse of McClellan before Richmond, Hill fought under Jackson and rendered major help to Stonewall Jackson at Cedar Mountain and Lee at Antietam. When Jackson was killed at Chancellorsville, Lee constituted and organized a third corps. In May 1863, Hill was made lieutenant general commanding the new corps, which led off the fight at Gettysburg. Hill, as a corps commander, manifested some psychosomatic problem and frequent lapses in generalship. His performance as a corps commander, unfortunately for the South, failed to measure up to his heroic deeds as a division commander. Here at Polegreen, Ambrose P. Hill found himself across the Totopotomoy from two of his classmates at West Point—Ambrose E. Burnside and John Gibbon. Seven days before the Appomattox Court House surrender, Hill was shot down by Federal stragglers near Petersburg. On Lee's deathbed in Lexington, Virginia, in October 1870, in his delirium, he called out, "Tell Hill he must come up."

John C. Breckinridge

John Cabell Breckinridge was a native of Kentucky, born near Lexington in 1821, and a graduate of Center College, a Presbyterian institution. He studied law at Transylvania University, practiced in Lexington and entered the Kentucky political scene, being elected to the legislature at twenty-eight years of age. At thirty-five, he was elected vice president of the United States. With a year and a half remaining in his term, the Kentucky legislature elected him to the U.S. Senate; however, when his home state failed to vote for secession and he was expelled from the Senate, he entered the Confederate army. In April 1862, he was promoted to major general. He was at Shiloh as commander

John C. Breckenridge. *Courtesy of the Library of Congress.*

of the Reserve Corps and later took part in the defense of Vicksburg, Mississippi, first in the summer of 1862 and then as a division commander in General Joseph E. Johnston's "Army of Relief" in the summer of 1863. Because the people of southwest Virginia expressed their displeasure over the repeated Federal cavalry raids and the poor performance of the Confederate commander in the area, in the winter of 1863–64, the Confederate War Department replaced Johnston with Breckenridge, who then carried out his operations in the valley of Virginia with two brigades. These troops, along with the cadets from Virginia Military Institute (VMI) and Brigadier General John Imboden's cavalry brigade, attacked Major General Franz Sigel at New Market on May 15, 1864, and drove him down the valley to the great relief of Lee, then engaged with Grant's forces at Spotsylvania.

At Lee's urging, Breckenridge and his infantry and artillery entrained at Waynesboro on May 18 for Hanover Junction. For the balance of the Cold Harbor Campaign, Breckenridge received his orders from Lee. In mid-June 1864, he joined Early in the defense of Lynchburg, to be followed by the raid on Washington. In February 1865, he was made secretary of war by Jefferson Davis. Following Appomattox, he went to England and Canada, finally returning to Kentucky in 1869, where he enjoyed great admiration from its citizens.

John Gibbon

Although wearing the U.S. insignia in 1864, Gibbon was a North Carolinian from Charlotte. He had accepted a commission in the army after graduation from the U.S. Military Academy in the class of 1847 and made a career of soldiering. Gibbon was much tougher and disciplined than many he commanded. He was deeply troubled by the problem of morale in the Federal army. In his *Personal Recollections of the Civil War*, he wrote:

> *Straggling from the ranks of the army during a battle had become so serious an evil as to excite the attention of everyone to its gravity. Immense numbers of men would quit the ranks upon the slightest pretext or none at all, leaving the more faithful to do the fighting and the shirkers, finding no serious attention paid to their absenting themselves, the evil continued and even increased. During the battle of the Wilderness, the roads behind our line of battle were literally filled with men, these improperly absent from the ranks.*

Gibbon addressed a letter to army headquarters and proposed that one out of every one hundred stragglers picked up by patrols be shot and that the percentage be increased in subsequent battles. The suggestion was not adopted, but shortly thereafter, General Grant issued an order from the headquarters of the Army of the Potomac authorizing summary court-martial for all deliberately deserting the ranks in battle. A few days later, a flagrant case of desertion came to Gibbon's attention, a trial was held, verdict issued and the prisoner sentenced to be shot. Gibbon recorded in his diary succinctly: "A straggler summarily tried today and sentenced to be shot at 7 a.m. May 20th, 7:08 a.m. He is just shot." The prisoner had been paraded in front of a firing party in the presence of the brigade to which he belonged, and with an open grave behind him, he was shot and buried.

A portrait of Brigadier General (major general from June 7, 1864) John Gibbon, officer in the Federal army. *Courtesy of the Library of Congress.*

This incident occurred ten days before the soldiers in blue and butternut deployed for battle near Polegreen.

Some years after the war, W. Roy Stephenson, son of a staff officer in Confederate major general Charles W. Field's command, wrote of his entertaining General Gibbon near Winchester, Virginia, on a hunting trip. The younger Stephenson had high admiration for Gibbon, as reflected in his account of two incidents that occurred during the war, one of which involved his father. He wrote:

> *John Gibbon was a North Carolinian, and had three brothers on the Southern side of that just quarrel. He was a West Pointer and, with George H. Thomas and other Southern-born officers in the old army, remained with his comrades in arms under the old flag instead of standing by his native State and people. While he was commanding a division before Petersburg, Va., he told me that he knew his three brothers were in the Confederate army before him, and he had heard that his dear old mother was very sick at the old home and would probably die. He sent a flag of truce with a note through the lines to his brothers asking about his mother's condition. He told me with grim humor that his brothers received his note and returned it by his messenger, saying that "neither his mother nor her sons recognized any kinship with a Yankee, and no communication with the family was possible until the matter in hand was settled." That happened a few days before Appomattox, where my father met General Gibbon at the McLean House. After the surrender there of General Lee and his army, General Gibbon was assigned by General Grant to parole the Confederate officers. He and Gen. Charles W. Field, of the Confederate army, were friends in the old service, and General Gibbon retained a very cordial feeling for his old comrade. After the meeting at the McLean House on the day of the surrender, General Gibbon, with several of his staff, rode to General Field's tent on the battlefield and provided him and his staff (of which my father, John Stephenson, was a member) with food and other necessaries that were then sorely needed. His kindness was never forgotten, and in after days he was a welcome visitor to our home in Virginia.*

The last forty-eight hours before the fatal day for Polegreen, Gibbon and his division looked across the Totopotomoy to a bluff and plateau beyond. About a mile in his front were the entrenchments of the Confederates. Within the next two days, these trenches were to be occupied by various units of A.P.

Hill's and Jubal Early's corps. One of Hill's division commanders, Henry Heth, is of particular interest to us, since he faced Gibbon on June 1.

At the echelon of division commanders, for the purpose of this book, particular attention is drawn to Brigadier General John Gibbon, commanding the Second Division of Hancock's corps, whose men fought back and forth across the Polegreen Church site for two days. Facing him during Polegreen's last day was Major General Henry Heth of A.P. Hill's corps. These two men were also graduates of West Point.

Henry Heth

Henry Heth was born in 1825 in Chesterfield County, Virginia, twelve miles southwest of the Confederate capital near Midlothian. His father, who had been a colonel in the Continental army, was the owner of the Black Heath coal mines. By the time Henry was ready for college, the family's financial condition had deteriorated dramatically, and he obtained appointment to West Point. There, he became friends with two other students—Ambrose

Burnside and Winfield Scott Hancock. At West Point, his friend Burnside on one occasion had entrusted Heth to attempt to patch up a broken engagement to marry, which had resulted from Burnside's getting drunk and falling out of a chair onto his fiancée's parlor floor. Heth pled Burnside's case to "Miss Nora" to no avail. He graduated from the academy in 1847.

Henry Heth, CSA. *Courtesy of Wikimedia Commons.*

Not long after the days at West Point, Heth and Burnside found themselves on duty in Mexico City, with the United States and Mexico at war. In Mexico, Heth was assigned to be aide-de-camp to Hancock and, as such, accompanied him on many "social" occasions involving beautiful Mexican women. Heth wrote in his memoirs of a later date in history:

> *In October, 1860, I received news of the illness of my child, whom I had never seen. I applied for a short leave, which was granted. Little did I think then that the next time I met my regiment (the 10th U.S. Infantry) and my company, in which I took so much pride, we would be on opposite sides of the field of battle…When I reached Fort Levenworth, everyone was talking about war, war. I ridiculed the idea of war; I was a strong Union man, and believed war was an impossibility. When passing through St. Louis, I found at the Planters' House a captain of my regiment, Captain John Dunovant of South Carolina, with a broken leg. Dunovant was saturated with the war fever; he was going to South Carolina, and if no other State seceded South Carolina would, and go to war if no other State did. I told Dunovant that in that event we would dig South Carolina up and throw her into the ocean. As I went east, war talk increased, and I became uneasy. A convention met in Richmond, strongly union in sentiment, but when the governor was called upon for 75,000 men, the convention suddenly changed its views and Virginia seceded.*
>
> *I had made up my mind that, in the event of my state, Virginia, seceding, I would cast my fortune with her. No act of my life cost me more bitter pangs than mailing my resignation as a captain in the United States Army, separating myself from those I loved, bidding adieu to my splendid company, my pride, and the finest regiment in the army.*
>
> *When Virginia seceded, April 17, 1861, so far as I know there happened to be but four officers of the United States Army in the State—Colonel Robert E. Lee, Major Robert Garnett, Lieutenant Edwin I. Harvey, and myself. I reported to Governor (John) Letcher for duty.*

Shortly after Heth joined the Confederate army, he became colonel of the Forty-fifth Virginia Infantry. He served first in western Virginia and then in Kentucky before he joined the Army of Northern Virginia and was assigned to A.P. Hill's division at Chancellorsville as a brigade commander. Heth led his division at the Battle of Gettysburg and was wounded, but he was able to recover rapidly enough to take part in all the subsequent battles of the Army of Northern Virginia. Henry Heth is said to have been one of two officers in the army who was addressed by his given name by General Robert E. Lee. At Polegreen, Heth's division was in the thick of the action on June 1, 1864. Heth must have considered it an honor beyond comparison that the beloved commander of the Army of Northern Virginia addressed him as he would a son.

William S. White

William S. White was the grandson of Captain William "Billy" White, Revolutionary War soldier. Captain Billy lived at Beaverdam, a home about a half mile east of Old Mechanicsville, overlooking Beaverdam Creek. (This was the site of the second conflict of the Seven Days Battles in the Confederate defense of Richmond in 1862.) Captain Billy's family were members of Polegreen Church, which was four miles northwest of their home. One of his sons, William Spottswood White, became one of the prominent Presbyterian ministers in Virginia. He was minister at the Presbyterian church in Lexington, Virginia, and was the pastor of General Stonewall Jackson. Another son, Philip, like his brother William Spottswood, was baptized at Polegreen Church. Philip named his son after his preacher brother.

Philip moved his family to Richmond, Virginia, in 1836, and his son, William, was born on June 24, 1840. When Virginia entered the war in 1861, William Spottswood was twenty-one years old. Without hesitation, he responded to the Southern cause and volunteered for the elite Richmond Howitzer Artillery. White maintained a diary throughout the war. His first combat was at First Manassas and his last at Appomattox Court House.

The diary of White records graphic detail of battles, camp life, exhausting days and nights of marching and numberless insights into his personal life and reflections on the meaning of those terrible times. He was heading toward the familiar country of his forefathers and into an experience of which the most fertile imagination could never have conceived.

James M. Aubery

James Aubery was born in Burlington, Vermont, on New Year's Day 1843, one of thirteen children. At eighteen, just before the war broke out, he finished the Burlington Academy. During his first job as a clerk in a general merchandise store, he caught the "war fever." Four of his brothers signed up in the Second Vermont Regiment. After the war had been going on for fifteen months, he could no longer resist the urge. He obtained several recommendations, one from the lieutenant governor of his state. It read, "Dear Sir: The bearer, Madison Aubery, of the town, is a young man of good habits, and active, faithful, and energetic. He is hardly stout enough for some marches, but he desires to do something for his country. I think he will make a good sergeant, or something of that kind. I hope you can find some place for him. I am yours, Levi Underwood."

Aubery was disappointed to learn, when he arrived at St. Johnsbury, that the regiment he wished to join had been filled. He then tried to get a job in the War Department in Washington but was turned down. The closest he came to being a soldier in January 1863 was to obtain permission to visit his brother in the Army of the Potomac, under Burnside's command at Belle Plain, Virginia. He wrote later, "My enthusiasm to get into the service, after being there a short time, completely left me. I soon learned that army life at the front was far different from what I had pictured it, which I had seen in the camps of the regiments while at home, and the marches, not what they were on the streets of Burlington." Aubery goes on to describe what brought about a change in his attitude about soldiering:

> I then and there concluded never to go into the army. I was there when General Burnside made his historic "Mud March" at Fredericksburg. At the commencement of the movement, the roads were good, but towards evening it became cloudy, in the night a cold "norther" came on, which made the roads as only Virginia roads can be, when considerably soaked. The red clay soil soon gets to such a consistency that the roads are almost impassable to even light vehicles. It was hurry, skurry, everywhere. Pieces of artillery, ordinarily requiring four or six horses, could not be moved with as many spans, the pontoon trains soon became almost immovable, men from the regiments were detailed to "put their shoulder to the wheel," with little success. The pontoon trains, artillery and infantry were literally wallowing in the mud. Men marching up to their knees in mud and water. Artillery wheels sunk to the hubs. Mules on the supply wagons floundering about. Wagoner's using their whips and the whole vocabulary of "swear words." Nothing but the ears of some of the mules could be seen, many literally drowned in the mud. Such was the "mud march" as it looked to me in January, 1863. I, as a civilian, fared better than the soldiers, or even than the generals, for I had but the responsibility of

myself and horse to make comfortable, as circumstances would permit, my whole worldly possessions being the horse, blankets and "dog tent," with plenty to eat, such as it was. I always had a square meal, for "hard tack" were plenty, they are square. But how different for those poor, wet, hungry soldiers. No writing can ever portray the suffering of those exposed to the elements of that famous "mud march."

In October 1863, James Aubery went to Milwaukee to visit a sister and said that there "the war fever came on me again." He enlisted on February 29, 1864, and was assigned to the Thirty-sixth Wisconsin Infantry, training at Madison, Wisconsin. Aubery maintained a diary of his time in service and later wrote a history of his regiment.

Chapter 5

Friday, May 27, 1864

By midday on May 26, 1864, General Grant had come to the same conclusion he had made each time he had engaged the Army of Northern Virginia since crossing the Rapidan. He had crossed the North Anna on the twenty-third, intent on a breakthrough that would carry him into the capital of the Confederacy, not twenty-five miles directly south. Now, again because of the stubborn resistance by Lee's Confederates, he was compelled to back off. Grant was abandoning a straight north–south shot at Richmond via the Richmond, Fredericksburg & Potomac Railroad and the Telegraph Road that paralleled it.

After dark, Grant ordered that his forces concentrate on the north side of North Anna. All night long, troops traveled back over both the canvas-covered and the sturdier wood pontoon bridges, as well as the Telegraph Road bridge, across which four days earlier they had marched south. Grant's intent now was the same as that previously employed—shift to the left (southeast) and attempt to turn Lee's right flank.

Grant had called up Major General Philip H. Sheridan from his activity southeast of Richmond to rendezvous with the advance units of the Army of the Potomac. The order had come when Sheridan's cavalry had reached Haxall's Landing on the James River below Malvern Hill. On May 17, he began his swing to the north, crossing the lower Chickahominy at Jones's Bridge, on to the Pamunkey at White House Landing and then northwest to Polecat Station, five miles south of Milford, where he rendezvoused with Brigadier General David A. Russell's division of the Sixth Corps of Meade's army on May 25.

The initial crossing of the Pamunkey was effected by Sheridan at Hanovertown, about seven and a half miles northeast of the Totopotomoy/Beaverdam Creek plateau, on March 27. He accomplished this without heavy resistance twenty-four hours before the main body of the Army of the Potomac arrived. Ira Spaulding, of the Fiftieth New York Engineers, reporting on the day's activity, wrote:

> *May 27th, the Reserve Battalion, with two canvas pontoon trains, accompanying General Sheridan's command, reached the Pamunkey at Hanovertown about daylight. Captain* [Martin] *Van. Brocklin, having the advance put a couple of boats together about a mile from the river, carried them to the river on the men's shoulders, and sent over the dismounted cavalry in these boats to drive away the enemy's pickets. This was done after a slight skirmish, and Captain Van Brocklin immediately commenced constructing his bridge, completing it in about one hour, assisted by Captain* [William W.] *Folwell and a portion of his company; length of bridge, 180 feet. General Torbert's division of cavalry immediately commenced crossing on this bridge. At 7 a.m. Captain Folwell constructed another bridge of 164 feet in length, a few yards above Captain Van Brocklin's bridge, completing it in about one hour.*

Two pontoon bridges positioned, Sheridan's crossing of the Pamunkey at Hanovertown took place on May 27 at 9:00 a.m. Lieutenant General A.P. Hill had dispatched the Maryland regiment under Brigadier General Bradley T. Johnson and Gordon's brigade of the North Carolina cavalry to the south bank of the Pamunkey at Hanovertown. These units engaged Sheridan but were pushed back down the Richmond Road toward Haw's Shop and thence toward Hanover Courthouse, 6 officers and 70 enlisted men being taken prisoner. Sheridan had the cavalry divisions of Torbert and Brigadier General David McMurtrie Gregg, totaling 8,000 men, with him. Brigadier General James H. Wilson's division was still up in the North Anna area. Added to that were 1,812 cavalry who were attached to Burnside's Ninth Corps. These nearly 10,000 cavalry pushed ahead the four miles to Haw's Shop, turned right and headed westward on the Richmond Road. Sheridan had already encountered Confederates in the area and expected more. How many more, he could not be sure.

In the early daylight hours of May 27, it was not clear where Grant intended to attack next, but that he would was a certainty. Movement of Union troops to the southeast indicated a crossing of the Pamunkey River somewhere. Thus, Lee ordered his army to withdraw from the North Anna, head south and be prepared for a new defense of Richmond.

While Grant himself was heading southeast to establish headquarters at Mangohick Church, on the north side of the Pamunkey not far from Hanovertown, Lee was riding south on the Telegraph Road in an ambulance with his mount Traveller unsaddled and following along behind. Confederate soldiers would have recognized Traveller and the implications of this scene. How serious was this matter? Lee had been hit at North Anna, not with a Minié ball but with an intestinal ailment that weakened him so much he could not ride his horse. Robert Stiles, one of Lee's artillery officers, remembered, "General Lee's indisposition about this time was really serious. Some of us will never forget how shocked and alarmed we were at seeing him in an ambulance." His Second Corps commander, Richard Ewell, was so sick with the same ailment that Lee ordered him to turn over command of his troops to Major General Jubal Early, the corps' second-highest-ranking officer. In a speech made after the war to the Confederate Veterans, Early said, "One of his three corps commanders had been disabled by wounds at the Wilderness, and another too sick to command his corps, while he himself was suffering from a most annoying and weakening disease. In fact nothing but his own determined will enabled him to keep the field at all; and it was there rendered more manifest than ever that he was the head and front, the very life and soul, of his army."

Around noon, Lee received word that some Union Cavalry had affected a crossing at Hanovertown. How close behind was Grant's infantry? He needed more information. There was not enough data at hand to deploy the entire army in defense of Richmond. What he did know was disturbing enough. There were not enough troops at his disposal to adequately defend against this adversary with seemingly inexhaustible resources. Interrogation of Union prisoners indicated a constant flow of reinforcements from the North. The policy of the North in granting citizenship to foreigners in return for their taking up arms against the South did nothing to prompt the Confederacy to capitulate. A Confederate soldier, writing in his diary of the Battle of Cold Harbor, expressed surprise that Union troops captured here could speak English because he had taken to the rear so many prisoners whose native tongue was German.

On May 27, Henry W. Halleck, chief of staff in Washington, sent the following correspondence to Grant:

HEADQUARTERS OF THE ARMY,
Washington, D.C., May 27, 1864.
Lieutenant-General GRANT, In the Field:
General: It appears from returns just handed in by General Christopher C.
Augur, that I have sent to Fredericksburg and Port Royal, since you crossed
the Rapidan May 4, a little over 40,000 troops. I hope within a few days
to send you between 5,000 and 10,000 more. As before stated, I have sent
to General Butler within the same period about 3,000. He telegraphs to me
today, that he will send with Maj. General William F. "Baldy" Smith to
White House Landing, 17,000 infantry. Some cavalry and artillery will
go with them, to cover the landing, escort trains, etc. I think he will make
the entire force about 20,000. This will make your entire reinforcements
since you crossed the Rapidan, between, 60,000 and 70,000 men. This
includes about 1,000 returned veterans, and 1,000 stragglers and deserters,
who have been arrested and sent back.

It is no wonder that Lee was concerned. While he was not privy to Halleck's correspondence, he could see the effect of such reinforcements. Herein it is indicated that in little more than three weeks, the Union army was bolstered with more reinforcements than Lee had in his army to defend Richmond against Grant in Hanover County.

As Lee continued south on Telegraph Road, his health didn't improve. It would take another four days before he regained strength enough to ride Traveller. In the meantime, there was a city to defend and an army to manage with two of his three corps commanders disabled. Ewell had Lee's ailment, and Longstreet had been wounded at the Wilderness on May 6 and replaced by General Anderson.

In late afternoon, Lee approached Sliding Hill Road, which branched off to the northeast from Telegraph Road and, a mile farther out, connected with Atlee Road, which he would take the next day. Inquiry at the Jenkins House, which fronted Telegraph Road about three hundred yards before it intersected with Sliding Hill Road, met with a hospitable response and an invitation to spend the night.

Grant's plan for crossing the Pamunkey called for crossing the river at two points, Hanovertown and New Castle Ferry, three miles downstream. But early on the twenty-seventh, trouble began to develop. Plans for an orderly withdrawal back across to the north side of the North Anna, which involved the removal of the pontoon bridges, destruction of the Chesterfield Bridge over the river to thwart advancing Confederates and movement of large numbers of men and large quantities of materiel, soon began to go awry.

At 2:00 a.m. on the twenty-seventh, Major General Winfield S. Hancock reported that most of the Second Corps had recrossed the North Anna and that he was ready to move out. Hancock was to fall in behind Wright's Sixth Corps, and Burnside's Ninth Corps was to get behind Major General Gouverneur K. Warren's Fifth Corps. But at 4:20 a.m., Hancock reported to the Army of the Potomac headquarters:

> *General: About an hour or an hour and a half ago General Burnside and myself understood that the roads were clear, and ordered a move; but while I was starting General Burnside received a message from General Warren, at his train, saying that it would be full two hours before his road would be cleared. I therefore halted. My road now is understood to be clear, but I am waiting for General Burnside to ascertain that his is also. The enemy show infantry pickets against us and occasionally a regiment, but I imagine no strong force, as they cannot cross the river very well. We hear nothing of our cavalry behind us.*

Elsewhere, another exchange of communications was taking place between Burnside and headquarters, in a far less pleasant tone. At 3:45 a.m., Burnside was asked by headquarters to explain why his troops had "cut the line of much of Warren's rear troops and the pickets of the Sixth Corps [Wright's] on the south side of the river." At 5:00 a.m., in response to this, Burnside took hot exception and all but demanded an apology from headquarters. Not until 9:00 p.m. that night was the matter addressed again. In so doing, the response of Grant's headquarters to Burnside's dawn message reveals an impatience with the Ninth Corps commander who had long resented being under the command of a man he outranked, General Meade. Grant wired Burnside regarding the incident:

> *May 27, 1864—9 p.m.*
> *Major-General BURNSIDE:*
> *The commanding general directs me to acknowledge the receipt of your dispatch by telegraph of 5 a.m. this day, and to reply to the same as follows: The commanding general is somewhat astonished that you should deem it necessary to repel insinuations on your veracity, as no such insinuations were ever designed. Nor does he deem the telegram sent to you obnoxious to any such charge. You reported the brigades of Maj. Gen. Thomas L. Crittenden's*

division in position and your corps ready to move, whereas, at that very moment a staff officer of General Warren was reporting to the commanding general that his pickets were delayed in crossing the river by being cut by a column of your troops. Now, while the commanding general is willing to admit the brigade could not reach Jericho without cutting Warren's column unless it waited for it to pass, and while he is perfectly satisfied with the explanation of the cutting he must insist the fact that this brigade was at that moment passing Quarles' Bridge, was inconsistent with the fact reported by you that it was in position at Jericho. This is all the commanding general intended to convey by the telegram. He is fully aware that you as well as himself are dependent on the reports of subordinates, liable to misapprehension and error and the knowledge of this, fact, he thinks, should have shielded him from the delusion you appear to have labored under that he intended to impugn your veracity or charge you with intentional misrepresentation. The report brought to the commanding general that some of your troops were on the south side of the river at that time was not well founded.

This would not be the last heated exchange between Burnside and his commanding officer. The frustration and fatigue of both men likely account in part for their reactions.

The delay in getting away from the North Anna, plus the weariness of the men who had gone at least thirty-six hours with no sleep, prompted Grant to change his plans about the location of the crossings of the Pamunkey. He first intended to send the Army of the Potomac across the Pamunkey at two points. The most eastward crossing was to be at New Castle Ferry, thirty-five miles downstream from the North Anna fight. Warren's Fifth Corps and Burnside's Ninth Corps were to cross at New Castle Ferry, and Wright's Sixth Corps and Hancock's Second Corps were to cross at Hanovertown. At 4:15 p.m., Grant's chief of staff notified Warren that Grant had changed his plans. He shifted the point of crossing back to the northwest, closer to Hanover Courthouse, abandoning the New Castle Ferry crossing, retaining Hanovertown and utilizing the crossing at Widow Nelson's Ferry, four miles west of Hanovertown.

The decision of Grant to allow the troops some rest and cross the Pamunkey early on the twenty-eighth was welcome. After skirmishing on the twenty-sixth, recrossing the river after dark and stopping and starting all day on the twenty-seventh, the men were exhausted. And it wasn't only the men who were tired. Casualties of war most often overlook the innocent and the helpless. Rarely are the animals even considered. Yet there is a touch of sadness to those who do care about such things. The report of Thomas

A. McParlin, medical director of the Army of the Potomac, gives a rare glimpse of this side of the war:

> *During the movement from the North Anna to the Pamunkey the ambulances and hospital trains moved in the same manner as in the march from Spotsylvania Court-House, a few ambulances remaining in rear of each division, and the remainder filled with slightly sick and wounded accompanying the main trains. The Cavalry Corps had by this time returned from the Richmond expedition, and two divisions moved in advance. A large number of the horses had become so much exhausted as to die on the road, along which they were scattered at tolerably regular intervals of from 50 to 100 yards, and the infantry following had the full benefit of the results of their putrefaction. This march of 30 miles was made rapidly over very dusty roads and on a hot and sultry day, and the number of men who fell out of the ranks was very large. All the ambulances were filled to overflowing, and a few men were unavoidably left behind.*

As the sun set on the twenty-seventh, Lee, with his headquarters being set up at the Jenkins House, sent a message to General Anderson that gives a clear picture of Lee's plans for the army for that night, as well as his strategy for the next day. Polegreen Church was now to be drawn inevitably into the center of conflict. The elevated plateau it occupied would be an objective of the opposing armies within a matter of hours. Lee's dispatch at 7:30 p.m. indicates why:

> *Headquarters Army of Northern Virginia,*
> *Jenkins' House, near Hughes' Shop,*
> *May 27, 1864—7:30 p.m.*
> *General Anderson:*
> *General: General Lee directs me to inform you that he will stop for the night at the above place. He wishes you to have your troops made as comfortable as possible for the night, and to move at 3 o'clock in the morning for Atlee's Station [sic]. General Early's corps is now near Hughes' Shop and will move at the same hour in the same direction. The object of the general is to get possession of the ridge between Totopotomoy and Beaver Dam Creek, upon which stands Pole Green Church. You will give Major General George E. Pickett all necessary instructions to join you in the morning. General Early's corps is just east of you and General Hill west of Pickett.*

There would be at least a few hours' rest on the night of the twenty-seventh for Lee's men. His adversary to the north, having delayed the major crossings of the Pamunkey River until early on the twenty-eighth, also allowed for the refreshment of his troops. It would not be a long night for the Confederates, as Lee had ordered them to march eastward toward Atlee Station on the Virginia Central Railroad.

William S. White, of the Third Company Richmond Howitzers, Cannoneer Fourth gun (Napoleon), noted in his journal:

> *May 26th.—This morning all quiet in our front. In the afternoon, the enemy attacked our sharpshooters in front of Daniel's brigade, and, for a short time, quite a spirited encounter took place; but we easily repulsed them, and again all is quiet.*
>
> *May 27th.—Early this morning it became apparent that Grant had declined a contest at Hanover Junction, and was moving his forces to our right, with the intention of occupying McClellan's old line near Cold Harbor. A corresponding disposition of our troops being necessary, we took up our line of march. Moving towards Atlee's Station [sic], our battalion camped for the night near that place.*

Along the line of march of the Army of the Potomac from the North Anna into Hanover County lay not only the usual debris of war—dead men and animals, broken wagons, lame cavalry mounts, discarded pieces of uniform, unneeded personal and military items, etc.—but also those other victims of war who were unfortunate enough to be in the path of an army advancing under orders to confiscate what was needed as food for soldiers and fodder for horses and mules. If anything else were left, it remained to the discretion of the men with the guns to destroy at will. Individual acts of compassion and mercy are to be found. Much more were the incidents of barns and houses burned, horses and cattle driven off with the passing army and families along the way left destitute. These helpless civilians experienced the understandable grief and resentment of those who saw ancient homesteads destroyed and a lifetime of work reduced to ashes. Large numbers of women experienced the fear and anxiety of trying to survive when their husbands, fathers and sons were in distant places serving their homeland.

A Union soldier in John Gibbon's division of Hancock's Second Corps tells of passing through an area that heretofore had escaped the ravages of war. Corporal John Day Smith of Company F, Nineteenth Maine Regiment, Colonel H. Boyd McKeen's brigade, described the passage of his comrades through that territory. He makes clear what the impact of their presence was on these noncombatants:

> At ten o'clock in the morning of the 27th, the Second Corps was off, and at ten o'clock that night the Regiment lay down on the ground about three miles from the Pamunkey, and nearly thirty miles from the starting point. Those who participated in that march, after the lapse of more than forty years, will recall that long, hot, dusty and tiresome march. It was through a region of country that had not been devastated by the tread of hostile armies, except occasional cavalry raids. The visible supply of fowls and pigs on the north side of the Pamunkey was greatly reduced during that day, and at many a farm house reluctant hands passed out from their scanty supply, food to the hungry soldiers. How good that food tasted! When the men inquired how far it was to Richmond, the spiteful reply would be, given by the women, in their peculiar Southern dialect, "It is so far you will never get there!"

The emotional trauma of men experiencing the early days of combat service is vividly described by James Aubery of the Thirty-sixth Wisconsin Volunteer Infantry. The first time he and his youthful companions had been exposed to the horror of war was five days before he crossed the North Anna. The awful sight of friends being torn asunder and the shock of viewing death firsthand were accompanied by the chilling sounds of the "rebel yell" heard for the first time. He described his experience at North Anna on the day of their withdrawal:

> While in the line of battle on the 27th a shell struck Company A, killing three and severely wounding four men.
> Killed—Privates Daniel A. Dibol and James C. McIntyre.
> Wounded—Corporals Marion A. Babcock, Geo. W. Ferris, Henry Oberweather; privates, Barber Palter, George G. Reeley.
> This was a terrible shock to the whole regiment, which was drawn up in line, just under the brow of a small hill, one wing resting higher up on the hill than the other. The gunner was a good one who could place a ball where he did; it was a solid shot. I shall never forget the horrible sight of one of the men who was hit in the loins. He walked to the surgeon and said, "For God's sake, doctor, can you help me?" It seemed worse than if it had been in a charge; it was murder. At the time the enemy was making a charge on our line, perhaps a half mile from us. We were listening to the "rebel yell." We could tell by the sound of it when they advanced and from it we could tell

that they were repulsed. We heard their "yell" die out and the cheer of our men. One who has ever heard that yell of the Johnnies will never forget it.

Says a writer in the Century: *"Life in the country, especially in the Southern country, where people live far apart and were employed oftentimes at a considerable distance from one another and, from the houses in which they slept and ate, tended, by exercise in communicating with one another, to strengthen and improve their voices for high and prolonged notes. A wider range to the vocal sounds was constantly afforded and frequently required.*

"The voices of women as well as men were often utilized for 'long distance calls.' It may be amusing to note the difference in intonation which was usually exhibited by the sexes. When a man had occasion to summon anyone from a distance, the prolonged tone was placed on the first note, the emphasis on the second, thus—'O, O, oh, John.' If a female called, the prolonged tone and the emphasis were both placed on the last note, thus—'You, John-ny-y-y.' Hallooing, screaming, yelling for one person or another, to the dogs, or some of the cattle on the plantation, with the accompanying reverberations from hill-tops, over valleys and plains, were the familiar sounds throughout the farming districts of the South in the days gone by. It used to be said by my father's old negro foreman that he could be distinctly understood a mile or more away. All of the 'high notes' and all of the 'emphasis' possible in the vocabulary were used in that devilish 'Rebel Yell' which we heard for the first time and which we were destined to frequently hear."

Chapter 6

Saturday, May 28, 1864

T hough Grant modified his plan concerning the Pamunkey crossings, Hanovertown continued to be a point of crossing for half the Army of the Potomac. But it was to be Warren's and Burnside's corps instead of Wright's and Hancock's. This little community, a century earlier, had been an important port in Virginia. The Pamunkey was one hundred feet wide here and deep enough to accommodate oceangoing vessels in the seventeenth and eighteenth centuries.

When one stands on the bank of the Pamunkey at old Hanovertown or on the Route 360 bridge over the river about seven miles to the east by water, it is difficult to imagine that oceangoing cargo vessels could have navigated this stream. Yet in 1676, Hanovertown, known as Page's warehouse, was the westernmost port on the Pamunkey, and ships from England often tied up there. Documents from that era tell that in tobacco shipping season, wagons and hogsheads were lined up for a mile, waiting to place their loads in warehouses at Hanovertown and also at New Castle Ferry downstream. One of the costs of indiscriminate planting practices in colonial Virginia was the extensive silting of its rivers and streams. The Pamunkey was one river whose seaports became unnavigable after a century and three quarters of abuse.

Haw's Shop was not a store. It was a manufacturing establishment run by the John Haw family, an institution in itself in Hanover County. The shop had a reputation all over Virginia and in other states for making quality farm equipment and milling machinery. The old Haw home place, Oak Grove,

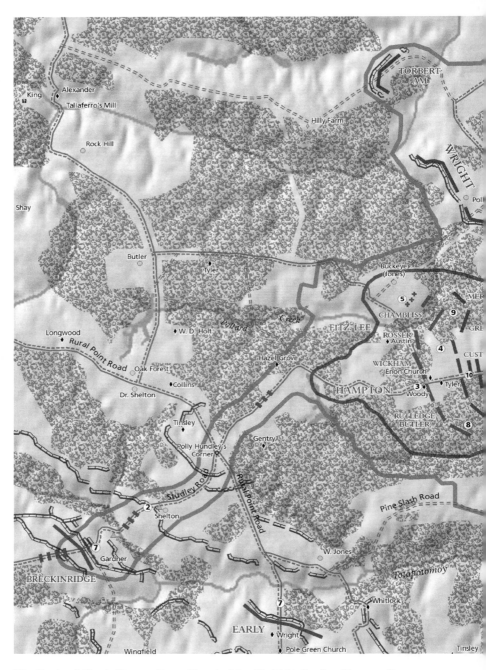

The Battle of Haw's Shop or Enon Church, May 28, 1864, Studley, Hanover County, Virginia. *Courtesy of the Library of Congress.*

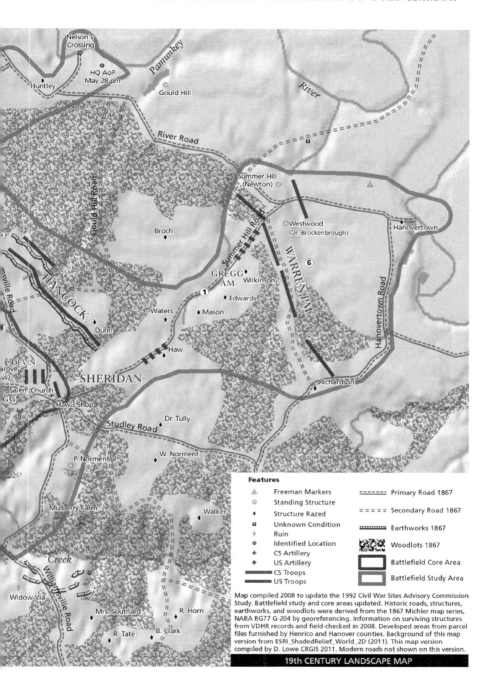

Features

▲	Freeman Markers	╌╌╌╌ Primary Road 1867
◎	Standing Structure	
◆	Structure Razed	═ ═ ═ ═ Secondary Road 1867
▣	Unknown Condition	▥▥▥▥ Earthworks 1867
◇	Ruin	
◉	Identified Location	▨▨ Woodlots 1867
+	CS Artillery	
+	US Artillery	▢ Battlefield Core Area
──	CS Troops	
──	US Troops	▢ Battlefield Study Area

Map compiled 2008 to update the 1992 Civil War Sites Advisory Commission Study. Battlefield study and core areas updated. Historic roads, structures, earthworks, and woodlots were derived from the 1867 Michler map series, NARA RG77 G-204 by georeferencing. Information on surviving structures from VDHR records and field-checked in 2008. Developed areas from parcel files furnished by Henrico and Hanover counties. Background of this map version from ESRI_ShadedRelief_World_2D (2011). This map version compiled by D. Lowe CRGIS 2011. Modern roads not shown on this version.

19th CENTURY LANDSCAPE MAP

had been built in 1783 and stretched one hundred yards on the north side of the road from Old Church to Richmond via Atlee Station. The Oak Grove home place had frontage on the Richmond Road extending one mile. On the east end, near the factory center, Haw had given the Presbyterians land for Salem Church, a daughter congregation of Samuel Davies and Polegreen. Earlier in the nineteenth century, the Salem congregation had its location at Hanovertown. By the Civil War, Polegreen and Salem shared the same minister. At the western end of the Richmond Road frontage of Oak Grove, Haw gave the Methodists land for the congregation at Enon. The Battle of Haw's Shop would involve all three of these buildings within twenty-four hours.

Early on May 28, when General Lee ordered cavalry toward the Pamunkey crossing at Hanovertown, the distance between his Jenkins House headquarters and Hanovertown was about fifteen miles. Major Generals Fitzhugh Lee's and Wade Hampton's men rode east on Atlee Road to Atlee Station and then out the Richmond to Hanovertown Road (now Studley Road/Route 606).

Later the same day, Lee moved his headquarters to a house near Atlee Station, about a mile north of the Chickahominy, a few hundred yards east of the road from Richmond to Hanover Courthouse. This brought him five miles closer to Hanovertown. He was invited into the Clarke House (Lockwood) and, in one room there, carried out his work as commander of the army. He was still plagued by the intestinal malady, or else he would have done his work in a tent, as he had done during the campaign since May 3. He was to remain at Lockwood until the afternoon of May 31. From Lockwood, he ordered the Second Corps to advance to Shady Grove Church and then two and a half miles on to Polegreen Church, which was only five hundred yards from the Totopotomoy basin. Behind and southwest of Early was Anderson's corps, followed by A.P. Hill's. From this position, Lee believed that if Grant chose to strike from the Hanovertown crossing anywhere along the Totopotomoy, he could defend himself along the bluffs overlooking the creek. Lee was well acquainted by now with this area of Hanover County. J.E.B. Stuart's reconnaissance from the June 1862 ride around McClellan, plus the battles at Beaverdam Creek and Gaines's Mill, had familiarized Lee with the area.

From the position Lee established on May 28, anchored at Polegreen Church, he felt that he could move to the left or right, depending on Grant's action. Should Grant attempt to swing around his own right and try getting into Richmond directly from the north down the Telegraph Road or the Hanover Courthouse–Richmond Road, Lee could reverse the Early-

Anderson-Hill line and easily cover the five miles back through Atlee to Telegraph Road. Should Grant follow the same course he had taken since crossing the Rapidan and continue his "sliding" action to the southeast in an attempt to turn Lee's right flank, Lee was ready for that also, as the first three days of June were to reveal.

As the Confederate cavalry rode out the Richmond-Hanovertown Road, which runs by Enon Church and Haw's Shop, they drew the fire of Sheridan's pickets straddling the road east of the church. Fitzhugh Lee's force had been strengthened by 1,100 South Carolinians who would soon see their first Virginia battle action. The Richmond Road in this part of Hanover County, to the west of Enon Church, ran through long stretches of heavily wooded pine trees and thick underbrush. A man could drive his animal fifteen feet off the road and be concealed. Fitzhugh Lee ordered his troops to dismount and, leaving their mounts and horse holders to the rear, form a line across the road to the north and to the south. A front was formed as the cavalrymen advanced from tree to tree and established a line at the church. To the east of the church along the road was much cultivated land interspersed with short scrub pines. From behind these trees and temporary breastworks of fence rails, the Confederates fought like foot soldiers, earning from Brigadier General George Armstrong Custer, later of Little Big Horn fame, the distinction of being "mounted infantry."

Sheridan's forces advanced and the battle was joined, lasting seven hours. Though it did not involve as many horses and men as the battle at Brandy Station, it was recalled by some as the fiercest cavalry engagement of the war. Many of the Federal cavalry were now armed with breach-loading repeating carbines that made for more rapid firing, plus much-lessened bodily exposure during reloading.

The Confederates still were using muzzleloaders. Robert E. Lee had observed that it was better for his army to stick with the muzzleloader, even if the newer weapons could have been procured. He felt the breach loader used up ammunition much more rapidly, and it was in short supply as it was. Secondly, he observed that soldiers using the slower-loading muzzle weapons would aim more carefully, thus offsetting the advantage of the enemy. But the muzzleloader did exact a price. Sergeant Robert Hudgins of Brigadier General William S. Wickham's Virginia brigade said after the battle at Enon Church that he "never saw so many men wounded in the arm in his experience during the war as in this fight."

During the early stages of the fighting at Enon Church, the Federal wounded were first carried into the Oak Grove kitchen, a large building detached from the main house that became the battlefield hospital. The medical director of the Army of the Potomac said in his report that "the medical officers of this hospital displayed great gallantry, as the building, at times, was under heavy fire, several shells striking the building, one falling under the operating table." Later in the day, the hospital was moved from the kitchen at Oak Grove a half mile east to the Salem Presbyterian Church and a nearby schoolhouse.

Among the many human-interest stories that can be related, two merit mention here. One of Robert E. Lee's greatest leadership losses in the war was the mortal wounding of General Stonewall Jackson at Chancellorsville in 1863. A second was that of General Stuart at Yellow Tavern on May 11, two weeks prior to the battle at Haw's Shop (Enon). While in the saddle, Stuart was mortally wounded by a Federal dismounted cavalryman. Writing of the May 28 fight, the commander of the Fifth Michigan Cavalry Regiment, Colonel Russell A. Alger, reported that his troops fought hand to hand in small pines to the left (south) of the road. He also stated, "I regret to report that John A. Huff, Company E, the man mentioned who wounded Gen. Stuart at Yellow Tavern, on the 11th of May, 1864, has recently died of wounds received at Haw's Shop, May 28th. He had belonged to Berdan's sharpshooters two years, and won the prize as best shot in the regiment. He was forty-eight years of age and lived at Armada, Michigan."

A second incident, one of compassion, is reported here as told by Joseph Q. Haw, son of John Haw of the shop:

> When Wickham's Brigade opened the fight, Lieutenant Harrod B. Christian led the advance guard, with his company mounted, and when near Enon Church the Yankees fired on them from behind a fence. Private St. George T. Brooke was shot in the thigh and left in the road. A Yankee put him in a fence corner and put a rail across to protect him from the tramping of the horses. He was carried to my father's yard with the Federal wounded. At the request of our family, when the Yankees carried their wounded to Salem Church, Brooke was left at the house. The next day Hancock's Corps passed up the road and the chief surgeon of the corps, Dr. Theodore James Calhoun, of New York, camped for the night in the yard. When told of Brooke's condition, he extracted the bullet from his leg and made him as comfortable as possible. He returned the next day from the front, four miles, bringing with him a wire splint to support his leg. A chaplain in the same corps, the Rev. Mr. Twitchel, of Maine, also visited him, bringing some lemons, a very rare luxury at that time. The latter gentleman was

an intimate college friend of Major Robert Stiles, C.S.A., at Yale. Brooke
recovered, but was always lame. He was professor of law for years at the
University of West Virginia, at Morgantown.

Stiles was a member of the Richmond Howitzers, who were on the south side of the Totopotomoy Creek on this day. After the war, he authored the book *Four Years under Marse Robert*.

While the battle raged, two other movements of troops north and south of the Totopotomoy were taking place. The encounter at Enon Church and the intelligence gathered from captured soldiers of Wright's Sixth Corps supporting Sheridan indicated that Grant's infantry had made a right turn at Haw's Shop toward the west, which alerted Lee to his next move. Grant was ordering too many troops toward Richmond to be ignored.

At Haw's Shop, Grant had two roads leading toward Richmond, one of which led south toward Mechanicsville and then to the Confederate capital. The other led west for three miles and then forked in three directions at Old Polly Hundley's Corner—not to be confused with Hundley's Corner, which was south of the Totopotomoy near Polegreen Church. At Polly Hundley's Corner, the Old Church–Richmond Road intersected the Hanover Courthouse–Cold Harbor Road. This intersection is the location of the present Rural Point Elementary School. At this site, two branches of the intersection are routed toward the Totopotomoy, both of which lead to Richmond. On the twenty-seventh, Lee had established an anchor at Polegreen Church with General Early's corps. Directly behind on the same road, Shady Grove Church Road, were Anderson's and A.P. Hill's corps. Lee had anticipated the possibility of Grant's move directly on Richmond. By late afternoon on the twenty-eighth, with the battle at Haw's Shop in progress, Lee exercised the option for which he planned. He directed Hill, Early and Anderson to establish a line along the bluffs overlooking Totopotomoy Creek. The left flank anchored five miles northwest of Hundley's Corner on the vital Virginia Central Railroad at Peaks. From Hundley's Corner, the line ran southeast, passing between Mechanicsville and Bethesda Church. A.P. Hill's corps manned the left of the front. Between Hill and Early was a gap that was covered by the Totopotomoy bluffs and thick woods. Next came Early's men, with Anderson held in reserve behind Early.

The Haw's Shop battle delayed the Federal advance long enough for the Confederates to dig in along the crest commanding the Totopotomoy. Picket lines posted in rifle pits were close to the creek itself. One line of Confederate rifle pits was established across the Polegreen Church yard. These can be seen today, although more than 149 years have passed. Lee had been trained at West Point in engineering, and most of his years in the U.S. Army had been spent in the elite Corps of Engineers. He was a master at evaluating and utilizing terrain as an element of his strategy. The battle fought along the Totopotomoy demonstrates how his forces utilized the combination of trench warfare and careful selection of ground to hold at bay enemy armies more than double their own strength.

During the battle at Enon Church, while Lee's infantry was digging in south of the Totopotomoy, Grant's forces were crossing the Pamunkey. His plan, when he withdrew from the North Anna, called for the Fifth and Sixth Corps to cross at New Castle Ferry, four miles east of Hanovertown and closer to Cold Harbor. The Second and Sixth Corps were to cross at Hanovertown. But on the afternoon of the twenty-seventh, Grant changed his orders and instead had the Second (Hancock's) and Sixth (Wright's) Corps cross four miles upstream from Hanovertown at the Widow Nelson's Ferry and the Fifth (Warren's) and Ninth (Burnside's) Corps cross at Hanovertown behind Sheridan. After the upstream crossing of the Pamunkey by Wright and Hancock, the former advanced along the road to Crump's Creek, and Hancock took the road to Haw's Shop. Warren, crossing the Pamunkey at Hanovertown before midday, moved on to Haw's Shop and crossed the Old Church–Richmond Road, feeling his way southward along the road to within a short distance of the Totopotomoy. Grant's orders for Sheridan to make a demonstration west of Haw's Shop on the Richmond Road concentrated the Army of the Potomac north of the Totopotomoy and demonstrated that by nightfall, he planned a breakthrough to Richmond from that direction. In his *Personal Memoirs*, with the advantage of hindsight, Sheridan summed up the intent of both Lee and Grant on May 28:

> *The most determined and obstinate efforts for success were now made on both sides, as the position at Hawe's [sic] Shop had become of very great importance on account of the designs of both Lee and Grant. Lee wished to hold this ground while he maneuvered his army to the line of the Totopotomoy, where he could cover the roads to Richmond, while Grant, though first sending me out merely to discover by a strong reconnaissance the movements of the enemy, saw the value of the place to cover his new base at the White House, and also to give us possession of a direct road to Cold Harbor…the battle was a decidedly severe one, the loss on each side being heavy in proportion to the number of troops engaged.*

The Battle at Haw's Shop ended where it started as far as terrain is involved. As dark descended, the shooting tapered off, and the Confederates, badly outnumbered, having accomplished their mission of delaying the Yankees long enough to enable Lee's infantry to take position south of the Totopotomoy, withdrew. As they held the field, the Union horse soldiers buried their dead. The Federals acknowledged the loss in killed and wounded at 350. The Confederates acknowledged 24 dead. There is today a small granite monument in the front yard of the Enon Methodist Church, marking the final sleeping place of 23 unknown Confederate dead. It is believed that most of these men were from South Carolina. Joseph Haw recalled:

> When the citizens of the neighborhood gathered up the Confederate dead, they found only twenty four [sic] killed in this battle and two killed on the 3rd of June, right at Haw's Shop. These they buried in Enon Churchyard, a mile below. The Yankees held the battlefield and buried their dead around Enon Church, which was between the line of battle, cutting their names on sides and back of the church and putting temporary markers over other graves. After the war, they were gathered up and buried in national cemeteries. The Confederate dead they placed in shallow graves (five South Carolinians in a washout), throwing a little dirt on them. After the war several parties came on from South Carolina to get the bodies of their dead, but only one party was able to identify the remains sufficiently to remove them. In 1866, Judge Robinson, of Columbia, wrote to General (Thomas M.) Logan, who in turn wrote to our family, to ascertain if it were possible to find the remains of his son. On inquiry of a neighbor whose house was between the lines of battle, we learned that they had seen a soldier's foot protruding from a shallow grave, with the name of Robinson marked on his underwear. These facts were written to the Judge, who came on to Virginia, bringing with him a young man who was in the same company with his son. This man said he could not identify the battle field, being so short a time on it, but that four of them behind a pine tree, two next to the tree on either side and two behind, these firing at the Yankees who were close up in some small pines. That he saw a Yankee aiming at them and told Robinson, who was immediately in front of him, to look out. Hardly had the warning been given when a bullet crashed through Robinson's brain, also striking him on the head and knocking him insensible. And he showed a scar marking the path of the bullet from front to back on top of his head. When the body was taken up, we found the skull pierced through and through by a bullet,

and found one gold filling in a back tooth. Not fully satisfied, the Judge returned home, but came back with his wife, who identified the body by the teeth and clothing.

At day's end, three of the Army of the Potomac's four infantry corps were strung out in a line from the Totopotomoy Creek crossing of the Haw's Shop–Mechanicsville Road almost to Hanover Courthouse, in accordance with Grant's orders. In response to Grant's movements, Lee, taking advantage of the time gained for him by his cavalry at Haw's Shop, positioned his troops on favorable ground south of the Totopotomoy, astride the direct route from the Pamunkey to Richmond.

William S. White, Third Company, Richmond Howitzers, recorded that during the "morning our battalion moved on the Old Church Road, until reaching the Cold Harbor Road, where we remained all night. We are about seven and a half miles from Richmond, but there seems to be no haste in the disposition of our troops, and the general impression is, that a decided battle is not imminent—some heavy skirmishing may take place, but nothing very important."

Chapter 7

Sunday, May 29, 1864

Late on the night of May 28, General Grant advised Meade's corps commanders to maintain contact at the flank position and be prepared for an attack by the enemy on the following morning. He had placed Wright (Sixth Corps) on the right, prepared to lunge toward Hanover Courthouse; Hancock (Second Corps) in the center, covering down to Haw's Shop; and Warren (Fifth Corps) on his left, holding the road from Haw's Shop to the Totopotomoy. Burnside (Ninth Corps) was to close up on this long line in the vicinity of Haw's Shop, act as a reserve and be prepared to move in any direction he was needed. Something needs to be said about the condition of the troops as the next phase of the Grant/Lee confrontation shaped up. Troops on both sides were bone-tired from forced marches from the North Anna battleground, marching day and night, at some places in knee-deep mud.

William Meade Dame, a nineteen-year-old cannoneer in the First Company of the Richmond Howitzers, described the conditions under which he and his comrades moved into position on the south side of the Totopotomoy in his book *From the Rapidan to Richmond and the Spotsylvania Campaign:*

> *Along about the 29th or 30th of May, we got on the march again; this time through the "Slashes of Hanover." It was an all-night march, and a most uncomfortable one. The rain had been pouring, and long sections of the road were under water. I think we waded for miles, that dark night, through*

water from an inch to a foot deep. And the mud holes! After a time our gun
wheels went up to the hub, and we had to turn to, there in the dark, and
prize our guns out; nearly lift them bodily out of the mud. I suppose we
did not go more than five or six miles in that all-night march, and by the
time day dawned we were as wet, and muddy, as the roads, and felt as flat,
and were tired to death. We halted for an hour or two to rest; then pushed
on, all day.

Dame was unsure of the dates mentioned above. As noted later, he was probably at least one day off, perhaps two. What he described was more likely events of May 27 and 28. The conditions, however, were accurately reported.

The Confederate soldiers were further weakened by lack of food. General Pickett, of Anderson's corps, reported to Lee at 1:30 p.m. on the twenty-eighth:

I have the honor to report my arrival at this point [Rose Cottage]
the men much worse for want of food, although but little straggling.
But in accordance with the suggestion of the major-general commanding
[Anderson], *I have halted here to wait for rations. In fact it is*
compulsory. It will be midnight, if not daylight, before we can get
anything to eat. The men are calling loudly for bread. I have sent 3
couriers and 2 staff officers back. We must get something, or the division
will be worse than useless.

The Federal commanders had to cope with a different problem—morale. Food, clothing, ammunition, reinforcements and transportation—all the things that enable an army to keep marching—were never a major problem for the Army of the Potomac. At this time in Grant's attempt to take Richmond or crush Lee's army, whichever he could do first, the troops that had crossed the Rapidan with him had suffered terrible losses in killed, wounded and captured. There had been scarcely a day since May 4 when fighting had not taken place somewhere along Grant's front. Both armies had experienced desertion by individuals. But straggling and desertion in the Union army reached a point on May 28 that, from the Fifth Corps, a circular was issued that stated, "The major-general commanding [Warren] directs that men found straggling away from the column be brought back by shooting at them." The next day, Brigadier General J.J. Abercrombie, commanding Union forces at Belle Plain and Fredericksburg, reported to Chief of Staff Halleck in Washington: "I omitted in my last telegram to report that between 400 and 500 contrabands [liberated slaves] were shipped last evening for Washington; also that I have picked up and sent to the front [Grant] over 2,500 stragglers."

> *HEADQUARTERS ARMY OF THE POTOMAC*
> *May 29, 1864—8 a.m.*
> *Brigadier-General* [Marsena] *PATRICK:*
> *GENERAL: It is reported to me that there are a great many stragglers recrossing the river at the bridges. You will immediately send a guard down to each of the bridges to arrest all such persons, officers, and men. Also send back some cavalry to bring up stragglers and communicate with General Wilson at Mangohick Church, and obtain from him any additional force necessary to drive up stragglers.*
> *Respectfully, yours,*
> *GEO. G. MEADE, Major-General*

At 8:45 a.m. on the twenty-ninth, Meade's chief of staff, A.A. Humphreys, laid out the objectives for the day, which were to become operational at noon. The order read:

> *First, Major-General Wright, Sixth Corps, will push out a reconnaissance with a division, artillery with it, on the roads running from his position to Hanover Court-House, and will support the reconnaissance with his whole corps if necessary. Second, Major-General Hancock, Second Corps, will in like manner throw forward a division, with artillery, on the road from Haw's Shop to Hanover Court-House, and support the reconnaissance, if necessary, with his whole corps. Third, Major-General Warren, Fifth Corps, will also push forward a division, with artillery, on the road to Shady Grove, and support it, if necessary, with his whole corps. Fourth, Major-General Burnside, Ninth Corps, will hold his corps ready to move to the support of either Hancock or Warren. He will send out a reconnoitering force, which will advance between the roads on which Hancock's and Warren's reconnaissance moves, and keep up communication between them and ascertain the ground between the two roads.* [This area was mostly wooded. Burnside would have had to cut his way through.] *Fifth, engineer officers and topographers will be assigned to each of the four reconnaissances to collect all requisite information.*

The enemy offensive that Grant anticipated on the morning of the twenty-ninth was not part of Lee's plan. Lee had succeeded by late night on the twenty-eighth by posting his available troops along a three-mile front south of the Totopotomoy along a ridge between that creek and Beaverdam Creek. Polegreen Church sat on that elevation alongside the Hanover Courthouse to Cold Harbor Road (present-day Route 643). At 5:00 p.m. on the twenty-eighth, while the battle continued at Enon Church, Lee ordered General Breckenridge to cover the road between Atlee Station and Haw's Shop, which was a main road to Richmond from that part of Hanover County. It is now called Studley Road. Breckenridge was further ordered to cross Totopotomoy Creek and move on another one and a half miles toward Haw's Shop. Water was available, Lee said, for Breckenridge's troops just north of the road over the crossing of Hanover Courthouse–Mechanicsville Road (present-day Routes 606 and 643).

By late night on the twenty-eighth, Lee pulled Breckinridge back south of the Totopotomoy. Pickets were posted north of the creek to keep in touch with the advancing Federals. Lee intended no offensive on the twenty-ninth. His orders that day to General Breckinridge state clearly his plans and give a reasonably accurate picture of the disposition of the forces available to the Confederate commander.

Lee's first message to Breckinridge, dated 6:45 a.m. on the twenty-ninth, read:

> GENERAL: *I do not propose to move the troops to-day unless it becomes necessary. I wish you, therefore, to get all your men together, rest and refresh them as much as possible, and supply them with ammunition, provisions, &c. Be prepared to move should circumstances require it. I think it probable that should the enemy intend to advance from his present position on Richmond it will be by Haw's Shop to Atlee's Station* [sic]. *I have directed General Hill to be ready to support you. Take a position to resist his advance, acquaint yourself with the roads and country in your vicinity, and post your pickets to insure* [sic] *your security. Advise General Hill* [at Shady Grove Church on the road from Atlee's to Mechanicsville] *as well as myself of any movement against you.*

At 3:30 p.m., some hours later, Lee replied to a midafternoon message from Breckinridge. The message drafted by Major Walter Taylor read:

> *GENERAL: Your note of 2:45 received. The general commanding directs me to say that General Early, with Ewell's corps, is on your right; he extends over toward Pole Green Church, and cannot be far from your right. Anderson* [Kershaw is a part of First Corps] *is in rear of Early, in reserve, and available for movements either way. The general does not think they will be able to or will attempt to pass between you and Early, but wishes you to be prepared and to hold the position you occupy. Have you your artillery with you?*

At 5:00 p.m., Taylor notified Breckinridge:

> *GENERAL: The last reports from the enemy represent him to be moving by Taliaferro's Mill toward Dr. Shelton's. General A.P. Hill is on the road from Shady Grove Church to Hanover Court House, and will advance to the point where it crosses Totopotomoy Creek. General* [William] *Mahone will be immediately on your left along the creek.*

Lee was concerned about the fatigue of his men, and unsure of Grant's intent, he chose to wait, rest and replenish with what resources he had available to him.

While Lee's army rested on the twenty-ninth, Grant's army was on the move, seeking to determine where to concentrate its attack when the time came. The Army of the Potomac's movements on this day demonstrated that Grant as yet had not chosen Cold Harbor as the point of a major attack.

What Grant did on the twenty-ninth was spend the day placing his troops to launch an attack from Haw's Shop toward Richmond. He established his headquarters at Haw's Shop and, the next day, moved it farther southwest, a half mile beyond Enon Church on the Richmond Road.

It is useful in appreciating the physical obstacles in the way of troop movements in this area of Hanover County to understand the terrain—the roads and the nature of the streams, marshes and, particularly, wooded areas. There are large areas in eastern Hanover County, known as the "slashes."

Henry Clay had popularized the ancient use of the term "slashes" by referring to himself as the boy from the "Hanover slashes." The word itself was commonly used to refer to those areas of ground frequently found in sections of Tidewater Virginia, including Hanover County, where the topography was such that drainage was poor. In these areas, during the winter and spring, the ground could be covered with several inches of water over large areas. Heavy growth of trees, particularly pine, grew in the slashes. Maneuvering an army, along with horses, mules, supply trains and artillery, through this kind of terrain was a major undertaking. Yet in Hanover County, it was frequently attempted.

In 1862, both armies fighting during the Seven Days Battles had difficulty with available maps. This was a devastating problem for men in an unfamiliar area. Troop leaders had to rely on the word of locals who were available to tell them where they were or the direction to certain objectives. In Colonel Ulric Dahlgren's February–March 1864 raid on Richmond from the west, down River Road, he became bogged down at a swollen stream. Assuming he had been intentionally misled by an African American guide whom he had picked up, he had the man hanged. By 1864, while both armies had their engineers develop more accurate maps, many still included inaccuracies. A unit of Lee's army reported having marched all night on roads south of the Totopotomoy and, at daybreak, found itself one mile from where it had started.

In addition to the problem of poor maps was the condition of the roads. They were narrow and built to accommodate a horse and wagon or carriage. Trying to move thousands of men and hundreds of pieces of artillery with supply trains along such a road became a logistical nightmare. Grant, faced with trying to get his army to the front, had to use what roads he could but also had to create some where none existed. This he ordered his corps commanders to do. On the Confederate side of the Totopotomoy, General Early had to do exactly the same in certain areas just south of Polegreen Church in order to attack Warren at Bethesda Church. Cutting new roads through thick woods and throwing up earthen fortifications, overnight in many cases, left troops exhausted before the firing of rifle muskets and artillery began.

On the morning of May 29, Grant was at his headquarters at Mangohick Church, five miles north of Hanovertown. He ordered General Meade to go ahead and join up with Hancock's Second Corps headquarters staff at Haw's Shop. The purpose was to learn as much as possible about what Hancock, and Warren in particular, were encountering in the way of Confederate positions and resistance.

The following exchange of communications between Generals Grant and Meade are given as typical of the dozens that passed back and forth as the advancing army sought to determine the location of the foe. I have edited them, as indicated by brackets, to illustrate or more clearly locate points of importance.

This photograph shows a group of Federal generals: Winfield Scott Hancock (seated), with division commanders (left to right) Francis Channing Barlow, David Bell Birney and John Gibbon. *Courtesy of the Library of Congress.*

HEADQUARTERS, SECOND CORPS,
[Haw's Shop]
May 29, 1864—3 p.m.
Lieutenant-General GRANT:
General Barlow [division commander in Hancock's Second Corps] *has advanced 3 miles on the road from this point and has reached the forks leading to Hanover Court-House and to Cold Harbor* [present site of Rural Point School]. *He has passed the scene of yesterday's cavalry fight* [at Enon Church], *1½ miles. He neither sees nor hears of anything of the enemy. From all I can learn I am under the impression the enemy has withdrawn behind the Chickahominy* [he probably meant the Totopotomoy, since the Chickahominy is five miles to the south], *but as yet this is only surmise. Nothing reported from General Wright or Warren. No firing heard.*
GEO. G. MEADE,
Major-General.

HAW'S HOUSE, May 29, 1864—3:30 p.m.
Lieut. Gen. U.S. GRANT:
General Barlow reports meeting a skirmish line of the enemy supposed to be cavalry. The people in the vicinity tell him there is a line of battle 1 mile ahead on Southard's Branch. Barlow is advancing to ascertain the true state of the case.
GEO. C. MEADE,
Major-General.

May 29, 1864—4 p.m.
Major-General MEADE, Second Corps Headquarters:
It will be well to keep the troops that have gone in search of the enemy to the front and close up on them in the morning, or, if you think their position unsafe, strengthen the front to-night. If the enemy has gone behind the [Totopotomoy] *the trains should all be brought to the south side of the Pamunkey in the morning. Your dispatch of 3:30 just received since writing the above. If the enemy is found in the position described by General Barlow, he had better be supported before making the attack. They are probably only covering whilst getting everything well ready to receive us on the south side of the creek.*
U.S. GRANT,
Lieutenant-General.

Haw's Shop, May 29, 1864—5:15 P.M.
Lieutenant-General Grant:
General Barlow has met the enemy in force about 4 miles from this point.
He reports artillery in position and infantry in rifle-pits. In accordance with
your dispatch I have directed General Hancock to support him, and he is
now moving out with his corps. General Griffin met the enemy about 1 mile
from the Totopotomoy on the road to Shady Grove, and is now skirmishing
with him. General Warren is prepared to support him. General Wright
reports his reconnaissance beginning within one-fourth mile of the railroad
[the Virginia Central]. *Hanover Court-House in sight; only cavalry*
pickets encountered. He will be directed to hold his advance position and
support them if necessary.

Geo. G. Meade,
Major-General.

At 10:45 a.m., the order to Burnside was countermanded, and he was ordered to hold his troops in reserve in the rear of Haw's Shop, ready to move to the support of either Hancock or Warren.

By the approach of dark on Sunday, the twenty-ninth, the Army of the Potomac had determined at least where its opponents were. At 2:50 p.m. that day, Barlow of Hancock's corps had advanced to Old Polly Hundley's Corner (not to be confused with Hundley's Corner on the south side of the Totopotomoy). It is now the crossroads where Rural Point School is located. Here he had encountered no opposition as he posted a brigade and a section of artillery and sent the rest of his division north (now Route 643) toward Hanover Courthouse. Encountering only Confederate cavalry, he returned to Polly Hundley's Corner and advanced on the two Richmond roads available to him, Atlee Road on the right and the road running by Polegreen Church on his left. As noted above, General Meade reported at 5:15 p.m. that Barlow had met Confederate skirmishers (Early's people) about a mile from the creek and was at that time engaged with them. This places the skirmish near the present location of the Rural Point School. This report must refer to action earlier in the afternoon, for fifteen minutes later, at 5:30 p.m., Hancock reported to Meade that Barlow

has found the enemy in some force on the Totopotomoy Creek [which
runs to the north farther than indicated on the military map

of that time], *about 1 mile from the junction of Cold Harbor and Hanover Court-House roads, where a line of works can be seen. The enemy Confederates appear to be moving to the right and left, manning their works. A contraband reports the road to Richmond "lined with troops," and says he counted twenty guns on the left of the road, in front of General Barlow. General Barlow has seen but three or four. I have sent word to General Barlow to make no attack, unless he receives further orders. His skirmishers are 1,000 yards or so from the works...The position of General Barlow is four miles from here* [at Haw's Shop] *on the Meadow Bridge Road. The map appears much at fault.*

The above report of Hancock to Meade makes it clear that Barlow, at Polly Hundley's Corner, proceeded toward the Totopotomoy by taking the Cold Harbor Road (Rural Point Road/Route 643) that passes Polegreen Church and, three-tenths of a mile beyond at Hundley's Corner, branches to the right to Meadow Bridge Road and to the left to Old Church Road.

At 5:15 p.m., Hancock had received a report that Brigadier General David B. Birney's division, which had marched from Haw's Shop during the day, that an infantry force was on his right. These were Breckinridge's troops, which Lee had sent out on the Hanovertown-Richmond Road (Studley Road/Route 606) to stop the Federals on that road to Richmond. In this same report, he said that Barlow was building a bridge over the stream. This bridge could have been a repair of the same one that Jackson used in 1862. It crossed the Totopotomoy on the Hanover Courthouse–Cold Harbor Road less than a half mile from Polegreen Church. Barlow's left flank rested on this road the night of the twenty-ninth. The 148th Pennsylvania was across the creek at this point by 5:15 p.m.

At 7:00 p.m., Hancock was ordered by Meade to bring the entire Second Corps to the front at daylight on the thirtieth. At the time the order was issued, Barlow was a half mile north of the creek along most of the line from the Shelton House (Rural Plains) on the Hanovertown-Richmond Road on his right, to the Hanover Courthouse–Cold Harbor Road, on his left, where the 148th Pennsylvania crossed the Totopotomoy. Birney was a half mile behind and to Barlow's right. Behind both Birney and Barlow, John Gibbon's second division was held in reserve. His division would play an important part in the Battle of Polegreen Church.

General Hancock gives a vivid picture of the situation on Barlow's right at Shelton's (Rural Plains) at 9:00 p.m. on the twenty-ninth. He wrote:

I have just returned from the front. When I arrived there I found General Barlow thought the position in front too strong for attack, and he had not examined sufficiently far to the right or left. I subsequently went down to the skirmish line and examined the position very carefully.

Just in our front there is an immense open space; a wheat-field, which extends also between Shelton's, in the center, and the creek. We have from the crest of this field near Shelton's a somewhat more elevated position than the enemy. They have epaulements for their guns, and two lines of rifle-pits as far as can be seen.

The banks of the creek, except at the crossing, are steep and abrupt, but not very high at the crossing, and indeed along there appears to be no obstacle to crossing owing to the stream; the high bluff and the enemy's guns apparently being the only obstacles. The enemy's troops did not attempt to conceal themselves. I should suppose there was a brigade there; from the smoke of fires some distance back, it appeared as if there were many troops there right and left. Our whole open space is swept by their artillery back to the Cold Harbor and Hanover Court-House road, where their shells fall. We can put batteries on that plain within 600 or 800 yards of them. The movements of the corps, to unite, ought to be made at the earliest hour; for if the enemy choose to cross and attack our isolated commands, it looks to me as if it could easily be done; the country is very open.

I placed Birney in line with Barlow; Barlow covering the road to Cold Harbor, and Birney that to Hanover Court-House. The lines of battle connect on the Richmond road. The enemy is working. They have some abatis about the crossing, it is so reported. They have at some points skirmishers on this side of the creek. I have ordered them to be driven back, wherever found in my neighborhood. Cavalry might to-night connect the corps, driving the enemy's cavalry and skirmishers across the stream. I shall direct epaulements for the batteries to be placed to-night within 600 or 800 yards of the enemy's, connected by rifle pits, as far as possible, in the darkness.

At 9:15 p.m., Barlow gave his assessment of his situation. He had by this time moved his headquarters, as noted on his order. This new location would have placed him at the crossroads near the present Rural Point School:

HDQRS. FIRST DIV., SECOND ARMY CORPS,
At crossing of Hanover C.H. and Cold Harbor road,
and road from Haw's Store to Richmond,
May 29, 1864—9:15 p.m.

COLONEL: I have the honor to report that I reached this point with my division at about 2 p.m. to-day. Driving in the few skirmishers of the enemy, I reached a point where the Richmond road crosses the Totopotomoy Creek. The western bank of the creek is held by the enemy in force; they have a line of works on the bank of the creek well filled with infantry in line of battle. In the part of the line which could be seen there were several pieces of artillery in the first line. In the rear of this first line there were several detached works and gun covers. One of these works contained two pieces and another one piece of artillery. I think there were three works, with two pieces each, besides single guns. There was a second line of infantry in line of battle.

I think their line crosses the Hanover Court-House and Cold Harbor road. [This was in the vicinity of Polegreen Church.] At least they have a strong line of pickets across the road about one mile from this point, and a force that I advanced against the pickets this afternoon received a heavy fire, and reported a line of battle. I shall inquire further in the morning. The enemy's lines of fire tonight are heavy, and extend on both sides of the Richmond Road. They are chopping, and apparently fortifying the line which crosses the Cold Harbor road. The Totopotomoy seems to be an insignificant creek, but the banks in our immediate front are steep. I think the ground on this side the creek commands the enemy's work, and that a heavy force of guns would render their line untenable, and enable us to cross. I have the honor to be, Colonel Barlow.

P.S.—I sent [John R.] Brooke's brigade this afternoon on the road leading from this point to Hanover Court-House. He communicated with pickets of General Wright on the road to Ashland. He found cavalry and a section of artillery but no great force. I could make no communication with Generals Burnside and Warren.

As Hancock prepared for the action of the following day, he ordered Colonel Tidball to put as many artillery batteries as practicable on the crest near the Shelton House. These batteries were to be well covered and connected by a line of rifle pits, which were to be manned by daylight of the thirtieth. What

Hancock was ordering was going to require yet another night with little or no sleep. Perhaps, without malice, he also was creating a situation by which Rural Plains (the Shelton House) would be a target for Confederate artillery emplaced on the south side of the Totopotomoy, a half mile away.

Something more descriptive deserves to be said about the Shelton House. It is a unique place for several reasons. Its history is rooted in the seventeenth century, and one of its remarkable features is that this American landmark has belonged to the direct line of Sheltons since it was built in 1670. The first Shelton obtained the property as a land grant, and it has remained in that family until recently conveyed to the National Park Service for inclusion in the Richmond National Battlefield Park. It is probably the oldest home in America to have remained in the same family since its construction. In 1754, Patrick Henry, future orator of the American Revolution, married Sarah Shelton in the living room of Rural Plains. The home sits about 150 feet east of the old Hanovertown-Richmond Road, a half mile north of the Totopotomoy. Since its first inhabitants entered its doors, it had never known a day such as it experienced on May 30, 1864.

As indicated earlier, when Wright (Sixth Corps) crossed the Pamunkey four miles northwest of Hanovertown on the twenty-eighth, he turned west and headed for Hanover Courthouse. The rest of the day, that night and most of the twenty-ninth, he advanced to the northwest and Hanover Courthouse by parallel roads, the northernmost emerging one and a half miles south of Hanover Courthouse on the Richmond Road. The road from Hanovertown to the courthouse is sometimes called the River Road (now known as Route 605). The road parallel to this emerges at Cash's Corner on the courthouse to Richmond Road, about two miles south of River Road.

By 7:00 p.m. on the twenty-ninth, Grant was satisfied that he faced no serious threat from Lee on the right flank of the Army of the Potomac. Furthermore, Barlow, of Hancock's Second Corps, had run into heavy opposition near the Shelton House on the road to Richmond (Studley Road/ Route 606), as well as the road from Polly Hundley's Corner by Polegreen Church (Rural Point Road/Route 643). The forced reconnaissance had convinced him that on the twenty-ninth, the greater part of Lee's army was south of the Totopotomoy on a four-mile front, running on a line from a mile west of the Shelton House by Polegreen Church to a point a mile and a half southeast of Polegreen. This placed Lee's extreme right near Bethesda Church. In response to this situation, Grant issued three orders. Wright was to leave a token force near the courthouse and bring the major part of the Sixth Corps down to the Totopotomoy and get on the right of Hancock's

Above: Rural Plains, 7273 Studley Road (State Route 606), Mechanicsville, Hanover County, Virginia, before destruction. *Courtesy of the Library of Congress.*

Left: Rural Plains, 7273 Studley Road (State Route 606), Mechanicsville, Hanover County, Virginia, after destruction. *Courtesy of the Library of Congress.*

Second Corps, in contact with Birney's division. Warren was to get his entire corps south of the Totopotomoy on the road from Haw's Shop to the Shady Grove Church Road (now called the Polegreen Road/Route 627). Burnside was to start moving toward the Confederate front, four miles away, and close the gap between Warren and Hancock. A look at a military map of the period indicates that between Burnside's position at Haw's Shop and his objective was a large dense woods. He was forced to cut his way through these woods to close the Federal front.

SUMMARY OF THE ACTION ON SUNDAY THE TWENTY-NINTH

For the most part, Lee's army dug in deeper and rested when it could. Much movement was taking place on the part of Grant's troops. There were more than 100,000 men massing northeast of the Totopotomoy Creek, twelve miles from Richmond. Between them and the Confederate capital was an army, ill equipped, hungry and outnumbered nearly five to three. Two of its three corps commanders were out of action: Longstreet wounded and Ewell down with diarrhea. Their commander, General Lee, was so ill with the same ailment as Ewell that he was directing his army during this day and for the next three from inside the Clarke House, three miles to the rear, near Atlee Station. Polegreen Church was less than a half mile from the front. Already a breastwork was thrown up fifteen feet north of the building. A line of rifle pits ran off to the southeast to Polegreen Creek, which empties into the Totopotomoy. Pickets manned these defenses.

Notice must be taken that on this night of May 29, Major General William E. Baldy Smith's Eighteenth Corps, Army of the James, was embarking from City Point east of Petersburg and twenty miles south of Richmond. Its destination was White House Landing on the Pamunkey.

William White of the Third Company, Richmond Howitzers, noted the following in his journal about the day:

> *Sunday, May 29th.—This morning our battalion moved on the Old Church road, until our troops are in line of battle, and awaiting the approach of the Federals. The severe lessons taught them at the Wilderness and Spotsylvania Courthouse, have made them more cautious, and they do not seem in any great hurry to run against Confederate breastworks.*

Chapter 8

Monday, May 30, 1864

G eneral, what is that firing?" Grant asked Meade's chief of staff, A.A.
Humphreys, at 7:15 a.m. During the night, the commanding general
had ridden westward from Haw's Shop about two miles on the road to
Richmond. He passed the scene of the battle at Enon Church between the
Confederate and Federal cavalry on the twenty-eighth and, a mile farther on,
set up his headquarters. This move was in the opposite direction from Cold
Harbor and indicates the intent of Grant on this date to "break through"
Lee's line rather than outflank it to get to Richmond.

Grant's headquarters were about midway between Hancock's and
Wright's corps to the west, and Burnside and Warren to the east. Warren
was engaged already on the left by Jubal Early, and Burnside had been
ordered to advance and close the gap between Warren and Hancock. The
firing Grant heard could have come from a number of positions. Hoping to
find out, Humphreys sent a message to Hancock, copied to Warren, at 8:45
a.m.: "The commanding general wishes to know what the artillery firing was
this morning a little after 7 o'clock."

General Hancock reported:

> *The firing this morning about 7 a.m. was the enemy opening on my working
> parties. My guns replied very little. I am waiting to complete my epaulements
> and the rifle pits for the infantry supports, when I shall open on their works.
> This is an advance work, and requires some protection for infantry in case
> it should be assaulted. The ground is open around, but could be assaulted*

if the enemy pleased. My rifle pits will be completed very soon. Barlow is pushing his skirmishers along the Cold Harbor road [Rural Point Road toward Polegreen, Route 643], *and is somewhat engaged. Gibbon will do the same.*

I wish to develop positively the enemy's position along that road. They have a strong line of skirmishers.

Hancock's report tells us that General Gibbon's division, which had been held in reserve on the Richmond Road to the east of Polly Hundley's Corner (east of Rural Point School), had moved during the early morning hours up toward the Totopotomoy and had formed on the east side of the road going by Polegreen Church. His orders had been to place his right flank touching the left flank of Barlow's division. Hancock's report also indicates that the Federals were running into heavy resistance within a half mile of Polegreen Church.

Two reports from Lieutenant J.E. Holland of Hancock's Signal Corps at 8:00 a.m. and 8:45 a.m. portend a day at the Shelton House never to be forgotten by its residents and their Hanover County neighbors. Holland first reported to Captain Peter A. Taylor, his chief, that the Confederates had fired on his working party with artillery from a distance of 750 yards, that the working party was throwing up earth protection for the Federal artillery and that brisk skirmishing was taking place on Barlow's front to the east of the Shelton House. Holland's second report is revealing. He had stationed observers (two, we learn from a later report) on the roof of the Shelton House. Holland modestly failed to mention that he was one of the observers perched on the roof. Their task was to direct the Federal fire. Their view was across the Totopotomoy about a mile in the rear and south of the Shelton House, where the Confederate line on this day was manned by General Breckinridge, former vice president of the United States and famous warrior from Kentucky.

At 9:40 a.m., Hancock reported that his patrols had connected with the troops of Wright's Sixth Corps who were marching down from Hanover Courthouse. If this contact was made halfway between Hancock's First division under Birney and Wright's most distant point from the line on the Totopotomoy, it would have been less than three miles from the front. Yet at 5:05 p.m., Wright's troops were just beginning to arrive. At 6:00 p.m., Hancock complained to Grant's headquarters that Birney had "remarked to me that the Sixth Corps had wasted hours in getting into position." Hancock also noted that his corps had been fighting for twenty-four hours without gaining ground, except that Birney's skirmishers on the extreme right had advanced toward the enemy to develop his position, as the Sixth Corps did not come up.

At 4:20 p.m., Hancock reported that Barlow, who was positioned along the Totopotomoy between the Richmond Road (Route 606, near the Shelton House) and the Cold Harbor Road (near Polegreen Church on Route 643), had advanced his skirmishers to the south side of the creek and had taken the first crest but that the enemy (Early's troops) held the hill beyond and commanded the crest occupied by his people. At 7:20 p.m., Hancock ordered his three division commanders— from right to left, Birney, Barlow and Gibbon—to assault at any point that might seem best. This order by Hancock came as a result of a plea for help from Warren on the Federal left, who was under attack from Early's corps near Bethesda Church. Thus Hancock's corps, by attacking on its front, would keep Hill and Breckinridge from sending reinforcements to Early in the area of Bethesda Church. Twenty minutes later at Grant's headquarters, General Meade ordered all operations to cease at dark, which allowed for at least another hour of daylight fighting.

Assistant Adjutant General Walker of Hancock's corps recalled in his corps history two unusual events at the Shelton home on this day. He wrote:

On the 30th [John R.] Brooke's brigade, which was deployed in front of Gibbon, supported by Owen's brigade, moved against the enemy's line of skirmish pits, and carried them in handsome style. These were immediately converted into cover for our own men. The enemy's position was found to be exceedingly strong—its front covered by the course of the Totopotomoy, much of the ground being marsh. The artillery was brought up and a large part of it placed in position along the ridge on which stood a large and handsome house [Rural Plains]. After a fierce duel Colonel Tidball succeeded in silencing the enemy, the range being unusually short. An incident of curious nature occurred in the yard of the house referred to during the artillery contest. One of the batteries had removed a limber chest for some reason, and while it was being filled with ammunition, a colored woman, crazy with fright, walked out of the kitchen with a shovelful of hot ashes, which she emptied into the chest. Two men were killed and others wounded by the explosion which resulted, the cause of the mischief escaping unhurt. In the army it always was the fool doing the mischief who got off safe. I have known several cases of soldiers opening shells, pouring out all the powder (they always pour out all the powder), and then dropped in a coal or match to see if there was any powder left. Out of all lives lost in this way I never once knew the original idiot to be injured. Speaking of the negro woman coming out of the kitchen reminds me that the house was occupied by its customary inhabitants during this cannonade, and recalls a somewhat amusing correspondence on that subject.

General Hancock, after deciding to attempt the passage of the creek, had instructed me to write to the ladies of the house immediately at the crossing, who, as he had learned, were then unprotected, informing them that their estate was likely to be the scene of a severe conflict the next day, and offering them transportation to the rear. This was done, and to save time an ambulance was sent along. In reply to the letter was received, an hour later, a very courteous appeal from the ladies not to make their house the scene of conflict; stating that one of the members of the household was sick and could not well be moved, and requesting that the Second Corps would take some other route. It being not altogether convenient to alter the plans of the Army of the Potomac at so short a notice, it was necessary to reply that the Second Corps could not well change its line of march, and that if they valued their lives they would retire. I not only sent the ambulance a second time, but requested the able and humane medical director of the corps, Dr. [Alexander] Dougherty, to visit them and see if the sick member of the household suffered no harm. Dr. Dougherty went and quickly returned. He had pronounced the sick lady to be in a condition to move without the slightest danger; but his opinion had been received with indignation not of the speechless variety. I myself received a letter, in which the opinions of the household concerning the President, Congress and the Army of the United States were set forth with the utmost distinctiveness. The epistle closed by informing me that if any of the family were killed on the morrow their blood would rest upon my soul forevermore. Inasmuch as the only possible chance of being injured was by shots from cannon manned by Confederates, it was difficult to apprehend the logic of this denunciation. The upshot was that the ladies, sick and well, stayed in the house, having moved down in the cellar. As our signal officers used the roof for purposes of observation the Confederate cannoneers were particularly attentive to it. The house was repeatedly struck, but none of the family in the cellar were hurt.

The first incident reported by Walker regarding the limber explosion is noted in the report of Colonel Morgan, who was eyewitness to part of the incident. His account reads:

In the Shelton house were several ladies who had refused to leave, notwithstanding the danger; they had taken refuge in the cellar and had with them a negress, who, when the fire was about the hottest, became delirious from fright, and picking up a fire shovelful of live coals from the hearth, rushed out into the yard and threw the coals into one of the limbers, exploding the ammunition it contained, killing 2 men I believe, and burning the eyes out of one or two others. The negress, who was unhurt, ran into the house again as if the devil was after her and nearly scared to death by what she had done. Colonel Brooke, Fifty-third Pennsylvania Volunteers, witnessed this affair with many other officers. I myself arrived on the ground just as the men whose eyes had been burned out were being taken off the field. It was not supposed that the negress had any intention of doing such mischief. She was so crazy that none believed she knew what she had done. (a note—I saw the tail end of this, but understood it was accidental; that the cartridges were on the ground and she threw the coals on them, and they in turn exploded the limber.—C.H. Morgan)

All during the day, the Shelton House drew attention from the Confederate artillery. By 3:30 p.m., Federal signal corps observer Holland reported that "the Shelton house is riddled by shot of the enemy. Our batteries and mortars in front of the house have silenced for the present enemy guns, our batteries doing splendid work, almost every shot striking where aimed. Slight skirmishing going on now." At the end of the day, General Hancock reported at 9:30 p.m. to Grant's headquarters the following:

My signal officers deserve special commendation today. Lieut. William H.R. Neel, Ninety-fifth Pennsylvania Infantry, and Lieutenant Holland remained at the station on top of Colonel Shelton's house during the whole day. The house was struck by 51 artillery shots, and both the officers were struck and bruised by shell. A large family of ladies were in the cellar of the house during the shelling, but I had last night advised them to leave, and did so repeatedly today, offering them facilities for so doing, which they refused, trusting in God, as they were members of the Church.

More than a century before, the Sheltons of Rural Plains had been among the followers of Samuel Davies at Polegreen Church, and after the Civil War, they were involved at Salem Presbyterian Church at Haw's Shop.

While the daylong artillery duel was taking place along the line of the Totopotomoy in the rear of Rural Plains on the Hanovertown-Richmond

Road, an all-out battle evolved three miles southeast in the vicinity of Bethesda Church on the Old Church/Richmond Road. Bethesda Church was east of the road, about two miles east of Mechanicsville. Warren's Fifth Corps, which had crossed the Pamunkey at Hanovertown on the morning of the twenty-ninth, had moved ahead a mile and a half to Haw's Shop, crossed the Hanovertown-Richmond Road and headed down to Totopotomoy Creek.

The road from Haw's Shop to Cold Harbor crosses Totopotomoy Creek, winds on down to Walnut Grove Road from Shady Grove Road, crosses Old Church Road (Route 360) at Bethesda Church and continues toward Cold Harbor. In the northeast quadrant of the Old Church and Walnut Grove crossroads (the present location of the Battlefield Elementary School) rested Bethesda Church. The battle that ensued there covered a radius of a mile around the church and bears its name.

On May 30, Warren came out of the southern watershed of the Totopotomoy and advanced toward Bethesda Church. The Federal cavalry to his front had already arrived at the crossroads. For hours prior to the movement of the Federal troops, Jubal Early had kept his troops busy cutting two parallel roads through the woods between Shady Grove Church Road and Old Church Road (Route 360), a distance of two miles, and had advanced his troops in the direction of Bethesda Church.

Early was sanguine about his ability to exploit the situation around Bethesda Church and proposed to Lee that his corps be allowed to attack Warren. Lee approved of the plan, as he had the other three corps of Grant occupied up the Totopotomoy for the moment, and allowed Early to use his own judgment as to the execution of the attack.

Early chose to employ Robert Rodes's division to spearhead the attack on his right. In the vanguard was the Forty-ninth Virginia Regiment, led by Colonel Edward Willis. The battle was hardly underway when Willis was killed and replaced by Lieutenant Colonel C.B. Christian. This regiment had lost nine color-bearers in the previous three weeks. The day was to be remembered by military historians as one of failure for the Confederates. Rodes's men initially pressed the Union forces back, but heavy and accurate artillery fire ripped the oncoming Confederates and compelled a retreat. But the day has also been recorded in Southern annals as an example of individual heroism and personal sacrifice. Many of the veterans of the Forty-ninth Virginia witnessed a scene they could not or chose not to forget. As the attack continued, Colonel Christian noted that the regimental flag was not displayed. Christian called out to a lad from Amherst County, Virginia:

"Orendorf, will you carry the colors?" "Yes, Colonel, I will carry them. They killed my brother the other day; now, damn them, let them kill me too."

Within moments, his words were to be etched in the memory of many of his comrades. Defiantly carrying his flag to within twenty feet of the Union line, he was blown to pieces by a cannon ball. Colonel Christian himself was, in that same encounter, wounded and taken prisoner.

As darkness approached on the thirtieth, General Gibbon sent Hancock word as follows:

> *The result of my attack, which was made at a very late hour this afternoon, was simply to advance the right of my skirmish line, well supported, to the foot of the bluffs on the other side of the stream, the tops of which were occupied by the enemy in rifle pits; not, however, in very strong force. The left of my picket-line, supported by a brigade, has swung around toward the right and moved up toward the right, for a time disconnecting itself from General Burnside's right, which I am informed did not advance. I have directed the connection to be re-established.*

The detail supplied by Gibbon is of particular interest in defining the Confederate defense line immediately around Polegreen Church. When soldiers of Gibbon's right wing crossed the Totopotomoy Bridge on the Hanover Courthouse–Cold Harbor Road (Route 643) and looked up at the Confederate rifle pits, they were only three-tenths of a mile from the church. A breastwork had been thrown up fifteen feet from the church, perpendicular to the road, running from the road eastward about three hundred feet. Diagonally from the area of the church nearest the road, a line of rifle pits was dug that extended downhill to Polegreen Branch, which empties into the Totopotomoy about a half mile northeast. This line was established to defend against the advance made by Gibbon, which he reported as his "left-picketline, supported by a brigade, has swung around to the right and moved up."

All afternoon on the thirtieth, reports were going back and forth between the four corps commanders and Grant's headquarters, as the commanding general sought to develop a continuous front with which to defeat the Confederate army. About the time he would get the flank of one corps in touch with the flank of another, a gap appeared between the two, and contact would be lost sometimes for hours. This was particularly true of the flank divisions of Burnside's corps and Warren's. Chief of Staff Humphrey contacted Warren at 6:20 p.m. to inform him that "General Burnside reports that he has connected with you twice today, and each time you have moved off your right without notice to him." At 7:45 p.m., Humphreys again sent word to Warren. Considering that the recipient was a graduate of the U.S. Military Academy, it is difficult to avoid what seems to be the tone of sarcasm in his message, which read, "The Major-General commanding [Meade] directs me to acknowledge the receipt of your dispatch respecting the connection with General Burnside, and to say that your orders required connection to be made with General Burnside before moving forward, and to be maintained during that movement, and that as a general principle the connecting flank shall never be moved without due and continued notice to the adjoining corps."

As noted earlier, Wright was slow in getting into place with his Sixth Corps on Hancock's right. It took him the entire day to move about four miles from the Hanover Courthouse area (a mile and a half south of the courthouse) down to Hancock's right on the north side of the Totopotomoy. By 7:00 p.m., Wright reported to Meade's headquarters as follows:

> *Notwithstanding constant exertion for several hours, I have but one division in position connecting with Hancock's right, and a second going in. The primary division is massed on the road protecting the right flank. The country through which the troops moved from the road is a swamp and tangle of the very worst character, and no possible effort could have got the troops sooner in position. The skirmish line report entrenchments in front of and a little to the right of the division in position.* [This was the entrenchment made by the troops of A.P. Hill]. *I have ordered the skirmish line well pressed forward, but it is too late to follow it up by an attack tonight. I have just returned from the line.*

Wright inquired of Meade at Grant's headquarters whether or not he wished a night attack. We may recall that Grant had ordered Hancock and Wright to launch an attack on the right to tie down Hill and Breckenridge so as to relieve the pressure of Early on Warren. Meade responded to Wright at 7:30 p.m. that he did not desire a night attack. Rather, he ordered Wright to mass all the force he had that was not at the front line and hold them in readiness to march. Grant now envisioned another shift to his left, a maneuver that had been employed since crossing the Rapidan four weeks earlier. Assistant Secretary of War Charles A. Dana noted during the afternoon that "General Grant means to fight here [at the Totopotomoy] if there is a fair chance, but he will not run his head against heavy works."

As darkness enveloped Hanover County on May 30, General Grant, in a dispatch to General Smith of the Eighteenth Army Corps, which had disembarked at White House Landing on the lower Pamunkey River, stated the disposition of Meade's four infantry corps:

> *The position of the Army of the Potomac this evening is as follows: the left of the Fifth Corps* [Warren's] *is on the Shady Grove road* [now called Polegreen Road or Route 627], *extending to the Mechanicsville road* [Route 360], *and about 3 miles south of the Totopotomoy. The Ninth Corps* [Burnside's] *is to the right of the Fifth; then come the Second* [Hancock's] *and Sixth* [Wright's] *forming a line, being on the road from Hanover Court-House to Cold Harbor* [now called Rural Point Road, Route 643], *and about 6 miles south of the Court-House.*

Grant also reported at 6:00 a.m. the following morning that his order to Wright, Hancock and Burnside at 7:00 p.m. on the thirtieth had been received in time for only Hancock's men to attack before dark. Thus, at dark, only portions of Barlow's and Gibbon's divisions of the Second Corps had gained a toehold south of the Totopotomoy on the right flank of the Army of the Potomac.

The few Confederate dispatches that were incorporated into the official record provide a sketchy picture of the activities along the lengthy front facing the Army of the Potomac. The "thin Gray line" was stretched to the limit and beyond at points. Indicative of this was the fact that most of the day a gap existed between Breckinridge's division, concentrated on the Hanovertown-Atlee-Richmond Road (Studley Road/Route 606), and whatever Confederate units were on his right near Polegreen Church. That morning, Jubal Early's corps was strung out from Polegreen Church two miles eastward to Bethesda Church, with Anderson's corps held in reserve. As things heated up along Shady Grove Church Road and near Bethesda Church, just east of the Old Church–Mechanicsville Road, Early had to pull his left division away from Polegreen Church, send it to the east and replace his left division with Charles Field's division from Anderson's corps.

Anderson reported at 8:00 p.m. that Field had "come upon an entrenched line of the enemy, and owing to that circumstance and the approach of darkness" his movement was being suspended and the line being pulled back to the left again so as to connect with General Breckinridge, "between whom and the left of my line a very wide gap has been made." At 10:00 p.m.,

Breckinridge reported to Lee's adjutant general Colonel Walter Taylor that Joseph Kershaw's division had been ordered away and that though he had sought troops to connect with his right, he had not found any.

What Lee had been compelled to do was substitute terrain and thick woods for troops along the line described above as a gap. Except for the daylong artillery duel around the Shelton House that required Breckinridge to stay in place, there were few Confederate troops in front of Barlow's division beyond the bluffs south of the Totopotomoy. Thus, along this one-mile line between the Shelton House and Polegreen Church, the men in gray were pickets and skirmishers. There was no battle line manned by infantry.

To the left and northwest of Breckinridge's brigades, A.P. Hill's corps at the end of the day faced portions of Birney's division (Hancock's corps) and a division of Wright's Sixth Corps, which was finally arriving. On the thirtieth, therefore, of all the troops at Lee's disposal, A.P. Hill was under the least threat. This also meant that he would be the next to be called on for support to the units down the line to the right toward Cold Harbor. The last recorded Confederate dispatch of the day was from General Lee's aide-de-camp Colonel Venable to General Breckinridge at 11:30 p.m. It read, "In case he [General Anderson] does not return before daylight, it would be well to protect your right with skirmishers, and notify General Hill, who has very little in front of his left, and can aid you."

As the day closed, Assistant Secretary of War Dana wrote Secretary Stanton a message that illustrates the waste and inefficiency of war. The complaint about Burnside evidences the lack of confidence in which he was held by the high command. It read:

> General Grant desires me to call your attention to an abuse which has existed at New Orleans, and possibly at Saint Louis also. When he took command of the Military Division of the Mississippi he found it in full bloom there. It consists in paying to officers who are lodged in the houses of rebels the regular commutation for fuel and quarters. He suggested that a general order be issued prohibiting such commutation in all the rebellious States. It is my duty to inform you that very serious mismanagement exists in the affairs of the Ninth Army Corps. The quartermaster's and commissary departments and the artillery alike suffer for want of necessary administrative authority. Animals are without forage and men without rations. It was to-day ascertained that the artillery horses of the whole corps have not had their harness taken off for the last nine days. Thus, in addition to the deficiency of their usual forage, they have

not been allowed to take any advantage of abundance of grass upon the way. In consequence of all this their shoulders and backs are sore, and they cannot last much longer. General [Rufus] Ingalls thinks that 1,000 new horses will be immediately wanted to supply the waste thus occasioned. General Meade has to-day appointed Lieutenant-Colonel J. Albert Monroe to serve temporarily as chief of artillery for the [Ninth] corps. He seems to have no power to interfere in the quartermaster's department. With regard to the rations the difficulty does not seem to lie with the corps commissaries, of which there are two, holding the rank of lieutenant-colonel, namely, Lieutenant-Colonel [Edwin R.] Goodrich and Lieutenant-Colonel [John H.] Coale, but, with the commanding officers, who have taken no measures to prevent their men from wasting their rations, or throwing them away. In fact, after the first battle [of the Wilderness], Burnside, instead of allowing his men to learn by experience the wholesome lesson that rations cannot be thrown away without suffering, issued to them 50,000 extra rations to make up those disposed of. These facts are known to General Grant, and I report them to you because I think you ought to be made aware of them also.

Dana reported that Burnside's corps finally got across the Totopotomoy on the evening of the thirtieth:

Diary entry by W.S. White
May 30th.—Some fighting was done along the lines to-day, by Early and Rhodes [sic]*, but amounted to nothing decisive."*

The activities of both armies during the day, which was typical of most of those in the campaign from the Rapidan to Cold Harbor, compels a certain degree of awe, particularly in regard to the fighting capacity of the Confederate army. Cataloguing the obstacles in the way of doing efficiently what soldiers are supposed to do when called into battle generates a respect not deserved by many armies. For four weeks, there had been a series of forced marches, frequently all-night affairs. When the men weren't marching, they were almost always digging. It is mind-boggling to think of how much dirt was thrown up into earthworks in Hanover County alone. From Peakes Turnout on the Virginia Central Railroad, there was nearly a continuous line, sometimes more than one, down to Turkey Hill below both Old and New Cold Harbor. The distance is about twenty miles. The amount of earth moved with anything available—from spoons and shovels to bayonets and canteen halves—is incalculable. Then there were those in great number who had not had any shoes issued for months. If they could not retrieve such from dead comrades or enemies left on the field of battle, they did without. The old adage about an army moving on its stomach breaks down when applied to the "thin gray line." Hunger was a constant companion. With little sleep, poor food or no food and physical exhaustion, one wonders how those men had the energy to fight. Yet they did, and they acquitted themselves honorably.

A Confederate of Breckinridge's division described the participation of his company positioned on the south side of the Totopotomoy, across from Barlow's division. T.C. Morton, captain of Company F, Twenty-Sixth Virginia Infantry, recalled:

That soon after getting in position, orders came for us to throw up breastworks in our front. There were few, if any, spades or shovels, but the men realizing the necessity for the order, as a heavy force was immediately in our front, split their canteens, making scoops of them, and, together with their bayonets and their hands, for the soil was light and sandy, soon had a very respectable earthwork thrown up, and lying down behind it, it was not long before we were all sleeping soundly. The next day…I received orders to take my company to the foot of the hill and occupy the picket line near the creek…The men concealed themselves behind trees, stumps and logs, or constructed hasty rifle-pits, and the enemy's picket line being on the opposite side of the creek, only partially concealed among scrubby pines and broom sedge, the opposing lines soon commenced a desultory fire upon each other, and it was not long before the artillery of the two forces engaged in the fight.

This cannonading soon grew heavy, and other batteries joining in from the opposite side, we found ourselves the centre of the most furious cannonading we had ever before experienced. There was no advance made by the infantry of either force during this heavy artillery duel, but it seemed as if all the gun and mortar batteries in Grant's army had been let loose on Breckinridge's devoted division. His few batteries responded with spirit, and returned the fire until they were badly crippled, while the infantry—not being brought into action and having nothing to do—cowered for protection from the death-dealing shot and shell in the piece of woods on our left, and behind every available defense. Many were killed and maimed, but the troops were not dislodged from their position.

I do not know what our loss was in this artillery fight, only recollect that two men in my own company were killed. One of them while lying down was struck on the back by a large piece of descending shell and cut in two, poor fellow. The other had gone to the rear a mile with a detail to cook and was on his way back to the line with a camp-kettle full of corn-bread and beef on his arm when the cannonading commenced. He ran towards the breastworks for protection, while the hungry men in the trenches watched his race through the ploughing shot and shell, almost as solicitous for the safety of their breakfast, perhaps, as for that of their comrade. Just before the poor fellow reached us, however, a shell exploded directly in front of him, and when the smoke cleared away the bloody fragments of the man and the scattered contents of the camp-kettle lay mingled together on the ground before our eyes. It is said that from the fullness of the heart the mouth speaketh, but on this occasion speech came from the emptiness of one poor soldier's stomach, when looking upon the ghastly wreck before us, he exclaimed: "Lor', boys, just look, Joe Hint is all mixed up with our breakfast, and it aint fit for nothing!" Such want of sentiment, or feeling if you like, sounds strange and heartless to us now, but in those times of courage and every day suffering, the hungry soldier's remark, finding an echo in the empty stomachs of his fellows, did not seem so much out of place.

Civil War casualties for the South in general, and for Virginia and Hanover County in particular, cannot be determined by considering the military alone. The cost to the civilian population was enormous, and for many families, the payment was unbearable. Some of the most descriptive and accurate accounts of the war's impact on noncombatants can be found in reports given not by the victims but by the victors. One of Meade's staff officers, Colonel Theodore Lyman, wrote of his observation of conditions in Hanover County on May 30, 1864:

May 30, 1864
It has been a tolerably quiet day, though there was a quite sharp fight at evening on our left—the Rebels badly used up. The people in Richmond must hear plainly the booming of our cannon: they scarcely can feel easy, for we are closing in on the old ground of McClellan. Fair Oaks was two years ago this very day. What armies have since been destroyed and rebuilt! What marchings and counter-marchings, from the James to the Susquehanna! Still we cling to them—that is the best feature. There is, and can be, no doubt of the straits to which these people are now reduced; particularly, of course, in this distracted region; there is nothing in modern history to

compare with the conscription they have. They have swept this part of the country of all persons under 50, who could not steal away. I have just seen a man of 48, very much crippled with rheumatism, who said he was enrolled two days ago. He told them he had thirteen persons dependent on him, including three grandchildren (his son-in-law had been taken some time since); but they said that made no difference; he was on his way to the rendezvous, when our cavalry crossed the river, and he hid in the bushes, till they came up. I offered him money for some of his small vegetables; but he said: "If you have any bread, I would rather have it. Your cavalry have taken all the corn I had left, and, as for meat, I have not tasted a mouthful for six weeks." If you had seen his eyes glisten when I gave him a piece of salt pork, you would have believed his story. He looked like a man who had come into a fortune. "Why," said he, "that must weigh four pounds—that would cost me forty dollars in Richmond! They told us they would feed the families of those that were taken; and so they did for two months, and then they said they had no more meal." What is even more extraordinary than their extreme suffering, is the incomprehensible philosophy and endurance of these people. Here was a man, of poor health, with a family that it would be hard to support in peace-times, stripped to the bone by Rebel and Union, with no hope from any side, and yet he almost laughed when he described his position, and presently came back with a smile to tell me that the only two cows he had, had strayed off, got into a Government herd, and "gone up the road"—that's the last of them. In Europe, a man so situated would be on his knees, tearing out handfuls of hair, and calling on the Virgin and on several saints. There were neighbors at his house; and one asked me if I supposed our people would burn his tenement? "What did you leave it for?" I asked. To which he replied, in a concise way that told the whole: "Because there was right smart of bullets over thar!"

The opposite of most of the deprivation experienced by the Army of Northern Virginia describes the advantage of the Army of the Potomac. Even so, the Union soldiers shared certain dimensions of war with their adversaries in gray. John D. Smith of McKeen's brigade, Gibbon's division (Second Corps), described on the morning of the thirty-first aspects of the day and night before. He had crossed the Totopotomoy close to Polegreen and had reached the plateau on which it stood. His record of May 30 at the close is vivid in its description of the thoughts and feelings of a soldier weary and frightened by what he saw and even more by what he could not see in the night:

The Regiment had been under constant fire all day from the sharpshooters. A welcome mail was distributed in the Regiment about dark. Early in the evening white rockets were thrown up by the enemy as signals, the import of which the men wished they understood. The entire Regiment spent all night on the skirmish line across Totopotomoy creek. It had been a hot, wearisome day, and there was some grumbling at the prospect for the night; but someone had to do the work, and the Nineteenth had been exempt from skirmish duty during the day. A comparatively quiet night was passed by the Regiment although the early hours were spent in cautious fear.

Intoxicated by the drugs of sleep, my eyes are heavy and yet strict vigils keep;

Imagination fills my drowsy brain with scenes of battle, fields of maimed and slain;

The stumps and bushes into phantoms grow, and shadows shape themselves into the foe.

Chapter 9

Tuesday, May 31, 1864

As the faint light of dawn slowly gave definition to trees and swamp, bush and field, the noise of chopping and digging continued until the morning sun was well above the tree tops, all along the front. At 2:00 a.m., the sound of Confederate drums beating reveille had roused the weary fighters on both sides of the Totopotomoy. Lee knew he did not have the troop strength to contend with the Army of the Potomac on anything approaching even numbers. Troop strength of officers and men present for duty numbered about 106,000 for the four infantry corps (Warren, Hancock, Wright and Burnside) and Sheridan's cavalry corps of the Army of the Potomac, and to all these forces soon would be added at least another 12,000 of Smith's Eighteenth Corps of the Army of the James, then disembarking at White House Landing on the Pamunkey. Grant had every reason to believe that he could, and would, crush Lee and his men along the Totopotomoy. Casualties numbered already in the thousands since the Rapidan had been crossed, and always there were men to be brought up to fill the ranks. There were also 242 Federal cannon on hand on the last day of May.

Lee faced that power with an army present for duty that numbered one-half that of Grant. Poorly dressed, poorly fed, short on weaponry and ammunition and with little hope of reinforcements, it is not surprising that some of the Yankees held this army in contempt. A Federal army surgeon, E. DeW. Breneman, reported on May 31 to Grant's chief of staff, John Rawlins, "From a few prisoners captured belonging to the Ambulance Corps of the so-called Confederate Army, it was learned the enemy were removing the wounded, theirs and ours…to Gordonsville and Richmond." Within three days from this dispatch, Breneman and his fellow surgeons would be dealing with overwhelming casualties being brought in from Cold Harbor, inflicted by that ragged enemy—the so-called Confederate army.

Lee, in anticipation that Grant would move toward Cold Harbor, had ordered a change in the disposition of his troops. There would be few men under arms on the night of the thirty-first in either army who had slept in the same place as on the night of the thirtieth. Having satisfied himself that there was little hope of driving his army through Lee's forces along the Totopotomoy, Grant set into motion the movement of his troops toward Cold Harbor. For many hours on the thirty-first, the men were shifting into a new alignment accompanied by the endless preparation of earthworks as new battle lines were formed.

Down the line from Polegreen Church, a mile and a half southeast in the area of Bethesda Church, General Warren's Fifth Corps was still engaged with Early's Second Corps. Lee felt it was imperative that he secure the position of his right at Cold Harbor, lest Grant turn it and interpose the Union army between the Army of Northern Virginia and Richmond. The cavalry fight between Fitz Lee and Sheridan at Old Cold Harbor, plus news that Union general Baldy Smith had landed his Eighteenth Corps at White House Landing and was headed toward Old Church, prompted Lee to remove Anderson's Corps from the Totopotomoy front between Early and Breckinridge. Anderson had been in the battle line running through Hundley's Corner.

The withdrawal of Anderson's corps from the center of the Confederate line created a situation that put every division of the Confederate army on the move during intervals when not fighting. Early shifted to his left, Breckinridge and Hill to their right, while Gordon's division of Early's corps moved all the way to its left to replace Field's division of Anderson's corps covering Hundley's Corner. These movements had the effect of thinning out the gray line even more than it had already been. Lee utilized the Totopotomoy swamp and bluffs and the thick woods on the plateau opposite Barlow's division (Hancock's corps) to defend territory where he was short of manpower. Reports of the Union commanders from all along the front, which now extended six miles, indicated major troop movements as well as continued throwing up of earthworks. The battle lines of the armies were so close at points near Bethesda Church that orders being shouted along the line could be heard by the enemy. Warren's forward patrols easily identified the sound of Confederate artillery on the move. These would have been Anderson's cannon as they were started toward Cold Harbor.

In Warren's effort to conform his line to contain any advance by Early between Bethesda Church and northwesterly toward Polegreen, he ordered Griffin's division to shift left (southwardly). As of 8:00 a.m., Griffin's division was north of the Shady Grove Church Road. As Griffin moved south of this road toward Bethesda Church, Burnside's men replaced the Fifth Corps soldiers, taking position between Hancock's and Warren's people.

Perhaps many wars produce those pathetic incidents when, on the last day of hostilities, some men are killed or wounded on the eve of peace. In times when communications were poor, some have been killed when the war was over. Something akin to this occurred at Bethesda Church on the thirty-first. This was to have been the last day in their tour of duty for a number of the Pennsylvania Reserves who were serving under Warren. Warren reported to Brigadier General Seth Williams at Grant's headquarters at 3:40 a.m.:

> *There has been considerable skirmishing going on last night and this morning where the dead and wounded lie, so that I have been unable to withdraw the Pennsylvania reserves till after daylight. I am afraid I cannot do it till after daylight today. They probably would not like to go until all their dead and wounded had been cared for.*

All along Grant's front, Lee's line was stretched to the limit and beyond. The only way to defend against a breakthrough by the Federals was to dig in and create a defense line of earth and felled trees that was impenetrable. Grant's first objective on the morning of the thirty-first was to test the enemy's defenses all along the front, in the midst of which sat Polegreen Church.

The seriousness of the situation that Lee faced is evidenced by his orders that troops spend much of the night digging in deeper and shoring up the line of battle with logs. Other communications also show his concern. Lee moved his headquarters from Atlee Station (the Clarke House destroyed in 1991) nearer the battlefront. On the thirty-first, his headquarters were at Coleman's on the road from Shady Grove Church (intersection of Meadow Bridge Road and Shady Grove Church Road) to Mechanicsville. From these headquarters, Assistant Adjutant General Taylor sent a circular to the corps commanders. The one to General Anderson read, "I am directed by General Lee to say that he wishes you to get every available man in the ranks by to-morrow. Gather in all stragglers and men absent without proper authority. Send to the field hospitals and have every man capable of performing the duties of a soldier returned to his command. Send back your inspectors with instructions to see that the wishes of the general commanding are carried out."

At 7:30 a.m., the first order of the day issued from Meade's headquarters near Enon Church read, "The (major-general) commanding directs that corps commanders press forward their skirmishers up against the enemy and ascertain whether any change has taken place in their front, and report the result." At 9:40 a.m., Hancock is asked the meaning of the firing taking place on his front. At 10:00 a.m., he responded to Meade's chief of staff that the firing was necessary to carry out the 7:30 a.m. order. Also, he reported that Barlow had possession of the first line of Confederate rifle pits for a distance of a brigade front (around six hundred yards) on the left of the Richmond Road (south, across the Totopotomoy, to the rear of the Shelton House) and that Birney's skirmishers on the right of the Richmond road had occupied the line (probably a skirmish line) that had been thrown up during the night. The Confederate troops encountered during this morning's action along Barlow's right and Birney's left were those of Confederate general Breckinridge. At 10:30 a.m., Birney reported that he had captured forty of Breckinridge's men and that the Confederate main line in his front was eight hundred yards ahead.

The left flank of Hancock's corps, under Gibbon, occupied the works to the left of the road from Hanover Courthouse to Cold Harbor, which was about seven miles to the southeast. Gibbon was close to Polegreen Church, forming an arc from just north of the church around to the east, with the church in his front. Hancock reported that Wilcox's division of Hill's corps had relieved Kershaw's brigade of Anderson's corps in front of Gibbon. This demonstrates that Hill had peeled off a division from in front of Wright's Sixth Corps and sent it two miles eastward to Hancock's left, near Polegreen Church. This placed Confederate skirmishers behind an extant breastwork, along an east–west line twenty feet from the church. A line of rifle pits led off at a forty-five-degree angle from the western end of the breastwork. These fortifications were to forestall efforts by Gibbon's people to come up through Polegreen Branch and attack from the northeast.

Hancock also reported that across this same road to Cold Harbor, Barlow's troops had encountered Hill's men. Sometime after 10:30 a.m., Barlow reported to Hancock that his left was confronted by a strong force with artillery that could not be dislodged without a heavy commitment by the Federals.

On the Army of the Potomac's right, General Wright and his Sixth Corps were having problems. At 9:30 a.m., Wright messaged Meade's headquarters to let him know what was taking place on his front. His description is vivid:

> *I respectfully report the result of the advance of my skirmish line as ordered this morning. The enemy appears to be strongly entrenched along my entire front, occupying a high ridge, difficult of ascent, and in some places perpendicular. The timber is slashed on the slope of the ridge, and immediately in front of the entrenchments (which are some distance back from the brow of the ridge) is an abatis. Immediately in front of my skirmish line is a swamp, thickly wooded, and averaging about 300 yards in width. The swamp extends to the foot of the ridge occupied by the enemy, and is occupied on the farther side by sharpshooters.*

At 10:00 a.m., Meade wrote to Wright that if he could not find an assailable point to his front, he should send out staff officers to learn the nearest roads and route to the rear of Warren's corps and then southeastward near Bethesda Church. In the meantime, he was to be prepared to advance in concert with Hancock and, if needed, to reinforce Hancock with troops from his corps. Hancock had maintained his headquarters near Polly Hundley's Corner. But as the possibility of a major effort at breaking through the Confederate lines loomed, spearheaded by his corps flanked by Burnside and Wright, he went forward to the Shelton House to be closer to the front. At 1:00 p.m., Hancock ordered his three division commanders to press the enemy "until he resists with more than skirmishers, and to establish a main line of their own on good ground."

By 2:10 p.m., Wright had all but abandoned the idea that he could make a successful breakthrough along his front. He notified Grant's headquarters that he was holding two of his divisions ready to support Hancock, if needed.

Heavy skirmishing went on all day along Hancock's front, and by 6:50 p.m., Hancock reported to General Meade: "I do not propose doing anything more tonight. My command is well deployed along the enemy's line—too much so to be concentrated easily. The two wings are across the creek [Totopotomoy]…and the skirmish line of the center, Barlow's division, but his line of battle could not be placed over without a fight of great disadvantage. I suppose I have lost several hundred men." With Gibbon's division across the Totopotomoy, it is probable that they had dislodged Wilcox's Confederates from Polegreen Church and had occupied their trenches. The main Confederate line southwest of the church, nearer Hundley's Corner, had held its ground.

The result of the day's effort from the Federal perspective was a repetition of what had been going on for the past four weeks. The Confederates, skillfully employing terrain, had added another day of frustration to the calendar of the Army of the Potomac in fending off a breakthrough to Richmond. By 9:45 p.m., Grant had made his decision, another "move to the left." This time, he called for Wright to take his Sixth Corps, pass behind Hancock and Burnside and take position in rear of Warren, near Old Cold Harbor. He was to be at Old Cold Harbor as soon after daylight on June 1 as possible.

With the change along the front occasioned by the redeployment of Wright, Hancock had to adjust his front to avoid an attack on his right flank by Hill's corps. If the Federals were not alert, Hill could shift his corps to the left, cross the Totopotomoy and attack Hancock's right, which was in the air. In making this adjustment, Hancock, at 10:30 p.m., ordered all his troops to return north of the Totopotomoy. A picket line would remain south of the creek. At 11:00 p.m., Hancock reported his action, which had put his troops back where they were in the morning. But at 11:20 p.m., Meade countermanded Hancock's orders and directed him to stay where he was unless "absolutely compelled to do so." When Hancock received this order, he responded:

> General HUMPHREYS:
> *Your instructions will be obeyed, but it will put my whole corps in a weak line; the two flanks being across the creek, and the center unable to cross, and with such an extended line, I cannot have any troops available for other purposes. The line I now hold is not of value, unless an assault is intended, and it is desired to mass troops close to the enemy. I can hold nearly the same ground, with skirmishers and artillery, from my old lines.*

What Grant had in mind was to keep as much pressure as possible on the Confederate defenses of Richmond on this flank of the line. What Grant did not want to happen was to allow Lee to move any of his troops (Hill's and Breckinridge's) from his left down toward Cold Harbor, as Grant had again decided to outflank Lee's right and interpose the Army of the Potomac between Lee and Richmond.

At 10:30 p.m., Wright began withdrawing his troops from A.P. Hill's front as quietly and unobtrusively as possible. One mile to the rear, they assembled on the Hanovertown-Richmond Road (Studley Road/Route 606) and marched toward Haw's Shop. Another all-night march was ahead. Sixth Corps soldiers had been up since dawn, digging in, maneuvering back and forth in front of A.P. Hill and skirmishing. Now they were to be ready to fight shortly after daybreak on June 1 down near Old Cold Harbor, seven miles away. Exhaustion was as formidable an enemy as the butternuts whose backs were toward Richmond.

Grant, having failed to break Lee's Totopotomoy line, notified his corps commanders at 11:30 p.m. that he was moving his headquarters. For the two days (May 30 and 31) that he had attacked Lee's center, Grant and Meade had maintained their headquarters west of Enon Church, some two miles behind the front. Focusing now southeastward, Grant rode during the night to Mrs. Via's house. He backtracked over the same road from Enon Church to Haw's Shop. When he reached Haw's Shop, he turned right and went south (present-day Route 615) on the Hanovertown-Mechanicsville Road for one and a half miles and, on the morning of June 1, set up headquarters at the Via House.

By correlating Hancock's May 31 6:50 p.m. report to Grant on the position of Gibbon's division with William Dame's (First Company Richmond Howitzers) diary and John Day Smith's (Nineteenth Maine Infantry) account, we have a good view of what took place around midday near Polegreen Church.

On the morning of the thirty-first, Gibbon assigned his three brigades these missions: McKeen's brigade was to cross to the south side of the Totopotomoy and prepare to advance up the slope, Colonel Thomas Smyth's Third Brigade was to remain on the north side of the creek as support for McKeen and Brigadier General Joshua T. Owen's Second Brigade was posted a half mile to the east of McKeen and Smyth. As Gibbon's left wing, Owen was to maintain contact with Burnside's Ninth Corps.

The south bluff of the Totopotomoy in Gibbon's sector and attack route did not rise as sharply as on Barlow's front. The Totopotomoy bottom was two hundred feet wide, shallow and thick with water lily pads.

At the time McKeen's brigade began its advance across the bottom, his ten regiments included three from Massachusetts, three from New York and one each from Maine, Michigan, Pennsylvania and Wisconsin.

Looking south from the Totopotomoy, McKeen's people saw a gentle wooded slope extending in their front for about two hundred yards. Rifle pits, now abandoned, dotted the slope. As the infantry advanced upward toward the clearing at the top, they crossed an abandoned picket line that ran along the edge of the plateau in front of them. This they occupied. Peering out of their line in the edge of the woods, Union infantry found themselves fronted by a wide cultivated field broken by the Hanover Courthouse–Cold Harbor Road. Five hundred yards in their front and just left of the road was a stand of ancient oak and ash trees. Along the southern edge of this farmland, where field joined the woods, were Confederate earthworks. Polegreen Church, a modest white frame structure, was in the woods, fifteen feet behind the earthworks. It had stood there since 1755, undisturbed and bearing its silent testimony to one of the great chapters in America's struggle for religious freedom.

When the Federals emerged from the woods on the edge of the Totopotomoy plateau and started across the open field and up through Polegreen Creek branch, the Confederates resisted for a while. But their skirmish line soon broke, and having lost some prisoners to the Federals, the remainder fell back to their main battle line, which ran through Hundley's Corner, a half mile farther southwest. For the next thirty-six hours, the breastworks, rifle pits and church itself were the focus of combat.

At midday, Gibbon sent skirmishers across the field northeast of Polegreen Church to occupy the building that sat in the grove. From the church and behind the trees, the Federals fired across the Hanover Courthouse–Cold Harbor Road and the farmland to the southwest. About 350 yards across this field, the First Company of the Richmond Howitzers, assigned to Anderson's corps, had taken position the evening before. Though Anderson's corps had been sent to Cold Harbor, the artillery unit was left in front of Polegreen until after dark on this day to give Wilcox's division support.

The Richmond Howitzers' William Dame reported that his company came up to Polegreen Church in the late afternoon of May 31. But Dame said he was unsure of the date. In fact, it was the thirtieth, which squares more with the Federal reports, as well as that of William S. White of the Third Company, Richmond Howitzers. Dame's account reads:

> *In the late afternoon we took our guns into position, on the far edge of a flat, open field. Two hundred yards in front of us, in the edge of a wood, was a white frame Church, which, some of the fellows, who knew this neighborhood, told us was "Pole Green Church." They also told us that the Pamunkey River was about a mile in front of us.* [The Pamunkey was five miles away. The Totopotomoy was less than a mile ahead]. *We heard artillery in various directions, but saw no enemy, and did not know anything of what was going on, except where we were. It was quiet there; so we went to sleep, and were undisturbed during the night.*

What he reports as having occurred the following morning actually happened on the thirty-first. He wrote:

> *The next morning we found that infantry had formed right and left of us, and we were in a line of battle stretching across this extensive field. About eleven o'clock skirmishers began to appear, in the woods, in front of us. They thickened up, and opened on us quite a lively fire. We stood this awhile until those skirmishers made a rush from the woods, and tried to gain the cover of the church building. Some of them did, and as this was crowding us a little too close, we took to our guns, and so doused them with canister, as they ran out, that they retired, out of range, into the woods. Soon after some infantry began to form in the edge of the woods as if they were about to charge us. We opened on them. They advanced a little, then broke in some confusion, and disappeared. The rest of this day, June 1st, along where we were, there was a lively sharp-shooting going on, up and down the line, and once a battery fired a few shots at us, but no special attack was made.*

Dame writes of artillery fire. Hancock had provided Gibbon with a fourth brigade of New Yorkers, four regiments of infantry and one of heavy artillery, the Eighth New York. The Fourth Brigade was stationed near the Jones House north of the Totopotomoy and remained there. The cannon shells fired at the Confederates had ranged about one mile. The Nineteenth Maine's Corporal Smith recalled:

> *On the morning of May 31st, the First and Second Brigades of the Division, preceded by a strong skirmish line, advanced to the top of the hill on the southwesterly side of the Totopotomoy, and about eleven o'clock in the forenoon charged, but the enemy's artillery opened with such effect that the line fell back a short distance and threw up earthworks. Colonel McKeen was in command of our Brigade. The rifle pits of the enemy's skirmish line were captured and held.*

The earthworks Corporal Smith cites as thrown up after the repulse are the same ones the Confederates had dug several days before.

As Dame reported, the Federals were soon dislodged from the church and forced back to their main line, these trenches being much nearer the church than those directly north. The church suffered some damage from Confederate canister, though not so extensive that it could not be used for the same purpose by Gibbon's men on June 1.

Dame describes an incident on the battlefield on that same day that gives a glimpse of another aspect of the conflict not usually described in official correspondence:

> *In the afternoon, taking advantage of the quiet, our negro mess cooks came into the line, to bring us something to eat. Each fellow had the cooked meat, and bread, for his mess, in a bag, swung over his shoulder. They came on across the field until within a hundred yards of the line, when a shell struck, in the field, not far from them. The bodies scattered, like a covey of birds! Some ran one way, and some another. Some ran back to the rear, and a few ran on to us. Our cook Ephraim, came tearing on with long leaps, and tumbled over among us crying out, "De Lord have mercy upon us." "Ephraim," we said, "what is the matter? What did you run for?" All in a tremble, he thrust out the bag towards us, and exclaimed, "Here, Marse George, take your vituals, and let me git away from here. De Lord forgive me for being such a fool as to come to sich a place as dis anyhow."*
>
> *"But, Ephraim," we said, "there was no danger! That shell didn't hit anywhere near you." "De ain't no use in telling me dat! Don't nobody know whar dem things goin'! Sounds to me like it was bout to hit me side my head, and bust my brains out, every minit; and if it had a hit me, dem other cooks would all a run away, and left me lying out dar, like a poor creeter." "But, my dear Ephraim," we said, "it mortifies us to see the 'Howitzer' cook running so, with all the men looking on." "Don't keer who looking! When dem things come any whar bout me, I bleeged to run. Dis ain't no place for cooks, nohow. Here gentlemen! take your rations; I got to get away from here!" We emptied the bag, he threw it over his back, and streaked with it to the rear.*

Even though, by most criteria, the Army of Northern Virginia was in a serious, if not desperate, situation as this day dawned, Lee made what may have seemed an unbelievable move. His men had spent three days and the better part of the nights establishing a defensive position south of the Totopotomoy. Now he made an offensive move. What made him do this? First, in spite of being outnumbered by the Army of the Potomac, the fighting on the thirtieth had assured him that his defenses were holding. Second, Fitzhugh Lee reported that Baldy Smith's corps had landed at White House and was marching toward Old Church. Third, this would be the best opportunity Lee had been presented since the North Anna to catch a significant number of Grant's troops on the move. If he could attack

Smith's infantry while they marched, he might drive them into Warren's left flank, create confusion and then order a general assault. If only Stonewall Jackson were alive!

To execute this plan, Lee, in midafternoon on the thirty-first, ordered Anderson's corps to move as quickly as possible to Old Cold Harbor, which was three miles southeast of Bethesda Church. Lee had finally persuaded President Davis to call up Hoke's division from Beauregard's forces that manned the Bermuda Hundred line. Hoke's four brigades were to join in the attack on Smith's corps. Anderson's withdrawal from the line in front of Polegreen would leave a gap between Breckinridge and Early. To close this gap, Hill and Breckinridge were to shift to their right. Early was to close to his left and seal the gap created by Anderson's departure. These movements by the Confederate units in front of Hancock's divisions created some confusion for the Federals.

About two o'clock in the afternoon, Gibbon ordered Smyth's Brigade to cross to the south bank of the Totopotomoy and be ready to support McKeen's brigade on June 1. This unit included two regiments each from New York and Ohio, plus one each from Connecticut, Delaware, Indiana, New Jersey and West Virginia.

Owen's brigade was also ordered to cross the Totopotomoy. This brigade numbered four regiments from Pennsylvania and one from New York. It was currently located about a half mile east of McKeen's people, near a road that also led to Cold Harbor via Bethesda Church. Owen's brigade faced a different topographical situation than McKeen's at Polegreen. South of the creek, the ground rose gently for a half mile before it leveled off onto a flat cultivated tableland. The field stretched for a half mile, at the south end of which the Confederates had thrown up strong works and cut down trees immediately in front to form an abatis.

Between nightfall and daybreak on June 1, the Army of Northern Virginia had been positioned for attack on its right flank at Cold Harbor by Anderson's First Corps, reinforced by Hoke's division. To Anderson's left, posted on a two-mile front, was Early's Second Corps, facing Warren's Fifth Corps from two miles east of Bethesda Church to the point where the Confederate line crossed the Shady Grove Church Road (present site of the Thirty-sixth Wisconsin monument). Breckinridge covered the front from there to the intersection at Hundley's Corner, where Jackson had bivouacked on the fateful evening of June 26, 1862. Heth's division of Hill's corps replaced Wilcox, connecting with Breckinridge at Hundley's Corner, and continued the battle line northwest, occupying the earthworks Anderson had vacated earlier in the day. To the northwest of Hundley's Corner were John R. Cooke's and William Kirkland's North Carolina brigades of Heth's division and then Mahone's division, extending northwest in front of Barlow and Birney of Hancock's corps. From Anderson's and Hoke's position near Old Cold Harbor to where Hill's corps anchored its left, the battle line extended seven and a half miles.

About midway along the line just described, Early's men had withdrawn on the thirtieth in face of heavy fire and losses to Warren's artillery. They fell back south of Bethesda Church and entrenched along a line crossing the Mechanicsville–Old Church Road (Route 360). Firing continued all day on the thirty-first, but there was no large-scale attack on the part of either army.

In support of Lee's left in the area of Polegreen, Hardaway's artillery battalion (Lieutenant Colonel Robert A. Hardaway), which included the Powhatan Artillery under William J. Dance, the Salem Flying Artillery under Charles B. Griffin and the Third Company of the Richmond Howitzers under Benjamin Smith Jr., was called up and attached to Heth's division. Like spokes in a wheel, this placed ten twelve-pounder Napoleon smoothbore guns and four rifled cannon within range of Polegreen Church, situated like a hub in the center of a battle line, which ran like a rim from three to five hundred yards south and southwest around it. It would require only one shot from a Napoleon to place Polegreen on the list of casualties.

Diarist William S. White of the Third Company, Richmond Howitzers, reported the movements of Hardaway's battalion on May 31 and June 1. The battalion's guns were called up to Hundley's Corner behind Anderson's First Corps on May 28 and were entrenched until the morning of the thirty-first, when they were limbered up and pulled back in reserve behind the line formed after the Confederate repulse at Bethesda Church. But after a respite that lasted only until dark, they were returned to the Hundley's Corner–Polegreen area. White wrote as follows:

> *May 31st—This morning our battalion was moved some distance farther on the right, and three companies* [Dance's, Griffin's and the Second Howitzer's] *were placed in position, whilst the Rockbridge Artillery and our company were held in reserve. We went into "park," on Mr. Cowardin's farm, "Liberty Hall," formerly owned by the Rev. Joseph Starke. This being in my old neighborhood, Lieutenant Carter and myself flanked out, and though the enemy are said to have taken everything from the neighborhood, yet we succeeded in getting a good dinner, consisting of fresh lamb, corn bread, sweet potatoes, Irish potatoes, butter, milk, &c. It was*

a God send to us! We are camped in a shady, pleasant grove, and that is much more agreeable than to be in those wearisome trenches. However, this piece of good fortune lasted only a short time, for at 7 P.M., our battalion, save the Rockbridge Artillery, was ordered to report on that portion of the line, near which we camped since the 28th, and relieve Longstreet's artillery, the First corps moving farther to the right. Our right extends to [Old] Cold Harbor, and our left to Atlee's Station [sic]. Longstreet's corps, commanded by Major-General R.H. Anderson is now on the right; Hill in the centre; and Ewell's corps on the left.

Major-General Jubal A. Early is in command of Ewell's corps, Ewell being quite unwell. Although the distance we had to march was not more than three or four miles, yet, having to move on private roads and through farms, it was nearly day when we reached our destination. Our two Napoleon guns (third and fourth) took position about three hundred yards in front of Pole Green Church. Our rifled section (first and second) was some six hundred yards on our right, and Dance's company to the right of it. Griffin's four Napoleon guns were a short distance to the left of our Napoleon section.

Often, military action between the North Anna on May 26 and Cold Harbor on June 2 has been largely neglected, being overshadowed by the terrible casualties on June 3. Yet Army of the Potomac chief of staff General A.A. Humphreys reported that Union losses alone, from the crossing of the Pamunkey through May 31, were already 3,022. While Confederate losses are unknown, they were probably at least half that number. The Union casualties reported by Humphreys did not include those sustained along the Totopotomoy in the action of June 1 and 2, prior to Hancock's attack at Polegreen and his subsequent withdrawal during the night of June 1 and 2. Additionally, the Totopotomoy casualties after May 31 were included in the Cold Harbor numbers. Casualties along the Totopotomoy for both armies would continue at least through June 3, when the Union general assault was launched.

Chapter 10

Wednesday, June 1, 1864

Disaster at Polegreen

ON WARREN'S FRONT

At 7:00 a.m., Warren ordered his skirmishers to press forward to establish contact with the enemy. Ninety minutes later, he reported to Meade that his corps was extended along a five-mile front, extending from Shady Grove Church Road a mile from Hundley's Corner down through the Bethesda Church area toward Old Cold Harbor. He could connect with Wright with no more than a skirmish line. Griffin was on the far right, touching the left of Burnside, and Cutler, in the center, covered Bethesda Church, with Lockwood on the left.

The better part of this day along Warren's front was spent in keeping contact with portions of Early's corps on his right and Anderson's on his left, a swampy area separating the two. No all-out attack by Warren was attempted. The same was true of the Confederates in front of Warren.

AT OLD COLD HARBOR

Lee had two main objectives for the day. Both focused on the vital Old Cold Harbor crossroads. Success in recapturing the crossroads would be a major accomplishment as Lee sought to strengthen his right to counter Grant's concentration of his forces on that end of the line. Lee hoped that by striking the Federals at daybreak with Anderson's men, who were supported by Hoke, he could retake the Old Cold Harbor crossroads and be ready to attack the Union Sixth Corps before it was reinforced by Smith's Eighteenth Corps and then press ahead on the road from White House Landing via Old Church.

The Confederate plan for the day began to unravel early. Though Hoke had been placed under the command of Anderson, he did not attack or contribute in any way to aid the effort launched by Kershaw's division of Anderson's corps, though he was well positioned to do so. The Union forces, under Sheridan, held the Old Cold Harbor crossroads. Wright's Sixth Corps had not yet arrived from the northwestern end of the line on the Totopotomoy. The Confederate attack was launched from Anderson's right, crossing the Old Cold Harbor–Bethesda Church Road in the vicinity of the D. Wooddy farm and Beulah Presbyterian Church. The debris of battle, including the burned church, unburied dead, field equipment and assorted evidences of combat, was in the path of the Union counterattacking forces in their effort later in the evening of this same day.

For some unknown reason, Anderson had chosen a relatively inexperienced regiment (the Twentieth South Carolina) that was not accustomed to combat waged at close quarters to lead the charge. The South Carolinians and their gallant commander, Colonel Lawrence Keitt, were not lacking in bravery, but when Keitt, mounted on his charger, was cut down almost immediately after the attack began, his troops fell back in disorder, hindering them from providing effective aid. In short, the Confederate attack was a disaster. It failed to retake Old Cold Harbor crossroads and preempted the opportunity to position the Confederate forces where they could attack the late-arriving Union Eighteenth Corps on the march.

It appears that Keitt attacked some works that had been built by Sheridan's men. Sheridan's 9:00 a.m. dispatch to Major General Humphreys tells of his having "captured more prisoners: they belonged to three different infantry brigades. The enemy assaulted the right of my lines this morning, but were handsomely repulsed. I have been very apprehensive, but General Wright is now coming up. I built slight works for my men. The enemy came up to them and were driven back. General Wright has just arrived."

Beulah Presbyterian Church lies on the eastern edge of the Old Cold Harbor–Bethesda Church Road (Route 633). It traces its history as a congregation to the ministry of Samuel Davies, who ministered to Hanover

County dissenters seven miles southeast of Polegreen Church. The church was built in 1836 by a congregation that developed out of prayer meetings in the David Wooddy home, which is adjacent to the church. Thomas Williamson Hooper was pastor of Beulah, Salem, Bethlehem and Polegreen Churches when the war began. He wrote:

> *In the campaign of 1862 the neat little church was used as a field hospital. The settees had been scattered through the woods by McClellan's forces, the windows were removed, the doors used for amputating tables, and the floor stained with blood. But in a short time we got the house in order, and resumed our services. These continued to the time I left, after Kilpatrick's raid, in 1864. In 1864 it was wantonly burned.*

Hooper went on to say that Polegreen had been destroyed in military action but Beulah had been deliberately destroyed. If this is true, it is likely that Sheridan's men set fire to it in the morning, for Federal troops of the Eighteenth Corps reported that they passed the smoldering ruins of the church in the afternoon.

Had the First Corps been under the wounded Longstreet, the story might have been different. Lee had hoped he would catch Baldy Smith on the road, unready for a fight. It was not an unreasonable expectation, as Smith had been given incorrect orders to send his corps to New Castle on the Pamunkey instead of Old Cold Harbor. This he did. He lost at least eight hours, and the extra distance that had to be covered on a severely hot day was punishing to his men. A number died of heat stroke on the dusty road, and the corps did not arrive and begin to form alongside Wright until 4:00 p.m., though Wright had arrived at Old Cold Harbor crossroads at 9:00 a.m. Even then, Smith came poorly prepared for battle. He failed to bring with him his hospital and supply trains and was almost without ammunition. Smith reported to Army of the Potomac headquarters as follows:

> *GENERAL: I have the honor to inform you that my line extends from the Wooddy house across the Bethesda Church road, partially along a rifle-pit, occupied by the enemy when I assaulted, the left brigade occupying a line of pits taken from the enemy today, making [a] line like a very obtuse V. On the right General [John H.] Martindale is spread out in one thin line without any reserves. The center, by General [William T.H.] Brooks, has a partial second line, his Third Brigade forming a second line to General [Charles] Devens, who is on my extreme left. I have already had the honor*

to report my necessities and requirements for ammunition, and having now given the present condition of my situation, must leave it for the general commanding to determine as to how long I can hold this line if vigorously attacked, one division being almost entirely out of ammunition, and one brigade of General Brooks having but a small supply on hand. Fearful that the note of mine to General Meade may have miscarried, I again state that I have one regiment armed with Austrian rifles, one with Sharps, and one with Spencer carbines. I am entirely without forage. I have not yet been able to ascertain the extent of my loss to day. I have to request that medical stores be sent to my wounded, as I had left before mine had been sent to me.

An aide to General Meade recorded his commander's reaction to the events of June 1 and, in particular, to the activity of General Baldy Smith:

General Meade was in one of his irascible fits to-night, which are always founded in good reason though they spread themselves over a good deal of ground that is not always in the limits of the question. First he blamed Warren for pushing out without orders; then he said each corps ought to act for itself and not always be leaning on him. Then he called Wright slow (a very true proposition as a general one). In the midst of these night-thoughts, comes here from General Smith bright, active, self-sufficient Engineer-Lieutenant [Francis U.] Farquhar, who reports that his superior had arrived, fought, etc., etc., but that he had brought little ammunition, no transportation and that "he considered his position precarious." "Then, why in Hell did he come at all for?" roared the exasperated Meade, with an oath that was rare with him.

When Smith reached the front near the Wooddy farm (three-quarters of a mile north of Old Cold Harbor), he was to have filled the gap between Wright's Sixth Corps and the left of Warren's Fifth. Yet another unusual occurrence took place along the Federal line. Division commander Lockwood of Warren's Corps had been ordered to form up Warren's left wing down toward the Wooddy farm. Warren reported to Meade on the night of June 1 the embarrassing incident that was to cost Lockwood his position as division commander:

General Griffin repulsed the attack on him to-night, which was no more than a strong feeler. The Cold Harbor road is not open, and I have been able to make no impression on the enemy. A very large field intervenes just beyond the forks of the road commanded by the enemy's batteries. I directed General Lockwood to extend well to the left with a line of skirmishers, and to prepare his whole division for an attack in conjunction with Wright and Smith. I thinned my line down to the least possible amount to get two brigades in reserve to support him, but in some unaccountable way he took his whole division, without my knowing it, away from the left of the line of battle, and turned up at dark 2 miles in my rear, and I have not yet got him back. All this time the firing should have guided him at least. He is too incompetent, and too high rank leaves no subordinate place for him. I earnestly beg that he may be at once relieved from duty with this army. Major [Washington] *Roebling has not yet returned.*

Lee had missed the last opportunity he would have in the war to engage the enemy by an offensive strike that presented a reasonable opportunity of success. But he was within thirty-six hours of the most successful defensive battle he would command in the Spring Campaign of '64—the June 3 Battle of Cold Harbor.

On Hancock's Front

Grant's decision on the thirty-first to shift his point of attack to the Cold Harbor area set in motion a redeployment of men and equipment. Up on the Totopotomoy were some fifty thousand men in the Union corps of Hancock and Burnside. As had been the case since the Army of the Potomac crossed the Pamunkey, Burnside was the least actively involved in the shooting. While he filled a gap between Hancock and Warren, he was positioned as a reserve for both. Hence, it was Hancock's corps that had been most involved in the action along the Totopotomoy since May 29. This pattern would continue throughout June 1.

Some portions of Hancock's corps would face men of four of Lee's commands sometime during the day. The shifting Confederate line south of the Totopotomoy would include regiments of Anderson, Early, Hill and Breckinridge. While Grant had shifted the focus of his effort to the left wing of the battle line, he well knew the risk of exposing his right flank. He would display his strength on the right for as long as he could, in the hope he could dilute the Confederate strength and keep occupied on that end of the line as large a number as possible of the men and boys in gray. In the case of the Second and Sixth Corps, Grant would underestimate the time it would take for both to march down to Cold Harbor at night and be ready for battle before daybreak.

The first dispatch of the day was sent from Humphreys to Hancock at fifteen minutes after midnight. It negated Hancock's suggestion of 11:50 p.m. that his corps be withdrawn to the north side of the Totopotomoy. Hancock felt vulnerable because of Wright's withdrawal from his right. The day's first dispatch set the tone for the Army of the Potomac's right wing. Hancock's role was to keep up the pressure on Lee's left flank, so as to keep his troops engaged and unable to be withdrawn and sent down toward Old Cold Harbor. The Battle of Cold Harbor, especially on June 3, has to be seen in light of the mounting frustration of Grant, who, after a month of continuous fighting from the Rapidan to the Totopotomoy bluffs, had been able to neither break through the Confederate line nor outflank it and move into Richmond. "Pressure Hill, pressure Breckinridge, pressure Early" was the meaning of the constant flow of dispatches all day long.

6:45 a.m.—Seth Williams to Hancock: "The commanding general [Grant] directs that you continue to press the enemy."

9:20 a.m.—Hancock to Meade: "I have ordered skirmishers to keep pressing the enemy."

10:00 a.m.—Williams to Hancock: "The commanding general directs that you push your skirmish line well to the right to notify you of any movement of the enemy."

10:00 a.m.—Meade to Hancock: "Hold your command in readiness to attack in your front. Warren and Wright [near Cold Harbor] will be engaged soon, and it may be necessary for you to attack to relieve them."

It did not take long for the Confederate left, under the command of A.P. Hill, to learn that Wright's Sixth Corps had withdrawn from its front the night before. The response to that was to send two brigades north across the Totopotomoy to get on the right flank of Birney's division of Hancock's Second Corps. Lee and Grant were engaged in a classic contest. Grant wanted to keep as much pressure as possible on Lee's left, to keep his troops tied down and not free to move off toward Old Cold Harbor. Lee wanted to keep enough pressure on Grant's right to take advantage of any opportunity that presented itself to attack that flank, roll it up and drive it down in front of his well-entrenched troops at Bethesda Church and Old Cold Harbor.

By midday, two decisions had been made by Hancock. The first was that the prospect of a successful assault by Barlow's division in the center of his line was dim. Barlow's skirmishers had ascertained that across the swamp the Confederates were firmly positioned, both in their skirmish line and in a battle line immediately behind that. Barlow's men at the front reported that the enemy troops had been chopping trees all night. Daylight made clear what all the tree cutting was about. The logs and dirt thrown up had created a defense almost impossible to penetrate, particularly as it was at the top of the bluffs that bordered the south side of the Totopotomoy and adjacent swamp.

Hancock's second decision was that an assault to relieve Warren and Wright would be most successful if led by Gibbon's division, which was on Hancock's left, with Gibbon's right resting on the Hanover Courthouse–Cold Harbor Road (Rural Point Road/Route 643). The attack would carry his troops through and beyond Polegreen Church.

As Gibbon advanced toward the Confederate line, the riflemen behind the trench at Polegreen and in the pits were driven out. Some were captured, as reported, from Wilcox's Alabama brigade. The main Confederate defense line was about four hundred yards to the west of the church in an open field.

At 11:00 a.m., Gibbon reported to Hancock:

> *Gen. Owens reports that his skirmishers are as far forward as they can go. He reports the enemy stronger than he supposed in his front and left front, and that his men are being killed and wounded in some cases in his line of battle. I have directed that, wherever it is practical, sharpshooters be pushed forward. The firing on Warren's front appears to advance.*

The attack on the Confederate lines, aimed at relieving Warren and Wright, prompted Hancock at 12:30 p.m. to contact Burnside, who was to his left and partially behind Gibbon: "If I attack I hope you will keep a close connection with Gibbon, as the attack will probably be on his right or on his front." Polegreen lay directly in front of Gibbon. At the same hour that Hancock was reporting to Burnside, Barlow was informing Second Corps headquarters of the state of affairs on his front:

> *I do not believe that these assaults upon entrenched lines through woods, where we do not know the ground, are likely to be successful where the enemy hold their line in force, but we will cheerfully try it if ordered. The enemy were chopping vigorously the whole night.*

Across the road from Polegreen and one hundred yards to the south stood the home of the Pollard family. Like the church, it was in the "no man's land" between the battle lines of the armies. Gibbon reported at 12:50 p.m. that a reliable officer of McKeen's brigade had seen "a battery of six guns on his [Gibbon's] right and front, which would take in flank any line advancing to my front, and which would, of course, have to be first taken…The enemy's works are just reported as well-filled with men since our sharpshooters have been pushing forward. The ground in my front is well swept by infantry and artillery." Shortly after Hancock received this dispatch, Gibbon reported that his skirmishers had gained possession of the Pollard House. The Confederate battle line angled sharply away from this home, which still stands and is occupied.

On Gibbon's front at 2:45 p.m., Confederate troops were seen behind their battle line, hastily moving to their left, in the direction of the Federal works that Wright had occupied. This gave Hancock concern because he was "not well-placed for a fight on that side." At 3:30 p.m., Gibbon was directed to make a demonstration supported by a line of battle to see if the Confederates were still in their works.

Also at 3:30 p.m., Meade sent a dispatch to Hancock that read, "You will make your arrangements and withdraw our corps tonight and move via Haw's Shop, to the rear of Bethesda Church. You will begin to withdraw as soon as it is dark. Notify Burnside when the last of your troops move and when you withdraw your pickets." This order was intended to bring Hancock's corps to beef up the attack Grant planned for dawn on the Confederate right fronting Old Cold Harbor.

General Owen reported to his commander, Gibbon, concerning the action of his Second Brigade a half mile east of Polegreen:

> *SIR: I have the honor to report that I sent out this morning 60 men under experienced officers with orders to advance as far as practicable, to obtain all information possible of the enemy's position and strength, and so to annoy him as to prevent his leaving our present front. I find that the enemy has concentrated his fire upon my left and left center, doing considerable execution, even in rear of my works, to prevent which I am now constructing traverses. The enemy's sharpshooters are in the open plain in front of his works, covered by sunken rifle pits. I am not able to annoy him much as I have no sharpshooters and but little cover of any kind in my front. His batteries are in the same position as yesterday and his strength apparently the same.*

That day, the heaviest action on the plateau between the Totopotomoy and the headwaters of Beaverdam Creek, with Polegreen Church at its center, came late in the afternoon. It was the second anniversary of Lee's assumption of command of the Army of Northern Virginia. From his headquarters at the Coleman House between Shady Grove Church and Mechanicsville, Lee was awaiting word of the action at Old Cold Harbor. It was to be his last opportunity to deliver a decisive blow at Grant north of the James with any hope of major success. But Hoke failed to coordinate with Anderson in attacking Sheridan's horse soldiers and regaining Old Cold Harbor preparatory to isolating Wright's corps. Hoke and Anderson had missed this opportunity to present their commanding general with an anniversary gift, which would have been appreciated. Lee saw through Grant's movements at the Confederate left and was confident that the enemy had no intent to wage an all-out battle along the Totopotomoy. Yet for those warriors on duty near Polegreen, the action was anything but a sparring effort. Viewed from the perspective of men who looked into the mouths of Napoleons armed with canister, what was taking place was no charade. Hundreds would be counted among the dead, wounded and captured. Personal diaries and regimental histories recorded their experience.

While all this activity with Hancock's troops was taking place, from predawn on June 1 until midafternoon, Lee's troops were likewise busy. Reports of moving troops to the left and to the right seem almost contradictory. Gibbon reported to Hancock that his men had observed units of the enemy marching in opposite directions. On the thirty-first, Anderson had been covering to the right of Hundley's Corner down Shady Grove Church Road to the present site of the Thirty-sixth Wisconsin monument, where his men connected with men of Rodes's division of Early's corps. Anderson also held the Confederate front from Hundley's Corner to Rodes's left, until they were in contact with Breckinridge. On his left were Hill's men. On the afternoon and evening of the thirty-first, Lee pulled Anderson out of the battle line and passed him behind Early to connect up with Early's right, extending the Confederate right toward Old Cold Harbor to meet the mounting threat. To fill the gap created by Anderson's departure, Lee had Early slide up to his left, Rodes's division being in the vanguard, followed by Gordon's division. Early again held the extended front between the Shady Grove Church Road to Hundley's Corner and connected with Breckinridge.

It was necessary for Rodes to move so far northwest to connect with Breckinridge so that Gordon's division covered the right and left of Hundley's Corner, with Hays's Louisiana brigade facing Polegreen Church.

When it became apparent to the Confederates that Wright's Sixth Corps had left the Totopotomoy after dark on the thirty-first, another adjustment was made. Lee ordered Breckinridge and A.P. Hill to start the shift to their right in the battle line. As Breckinridge began to move toward Hundley's Corner, Rodes's men vacated the battle line and formed up about three hundred yards behind the main line near Shady Grove Church Road to the southwest. They were in the same field that had been occupied by part of Jackson's corps on the night of June 26, 1862, while Lee was waiting for him at Mechanicsville. As Breckinridge continued eastward, Gordon shifted to his right to make way. Thus, for several hours, Rodes was held in reserve behind John Cooke's and William W. Kirkland's brigades of Heth's division. Heth had settled in at noon on the first at Hundley's Corner and in front of Polegreen. Breckinridge was posted from Hundley's Corner along Shady Grove Church Road to the point where the Confederate line turned south, crossing the road. Thus, Breckinridge connected with Gordon's division (Early's corps).

The First Company of the Richmond Howitzers had been with Anderson's corps while he was in front of Polegreen on the thirtieth and thirty-first. They marched off with him during the early morning hours of June 1 and were replaced by the Third Company of the Richmond Howitzers.

Across the fields to the south and west of Polegreen Church, the Confederates faced McKeen's brigade, backed up by Smyth's brigade of Gibbon's division. To their right, the ground was occupied by John R. Brooke's brigade of Barlow's division.

June 1 was a hot and dry day in Hanover County. There had been heavy rain on May 29, enough to create problems for the men and equipment on the muddy roads south of the North Anna. The soil in eastern Hanover County contains large amounts of sand, and moisture leaches rapidly. On hot sunny days, the surface can easily become dusty in twenty-four to thirty-six hours. Men fighting at Polegreen reported great discomfort on this day, noting the dust clouds created by running men and the impact of cannon shot and Minié balls striking the ground.

At 4:30 p.m., the Federal thrust toward the Confederate line began. From the cover of woods near Polegreen, the men of McKeen's brigade began their advance toward the entrenched Confederate battle line. Four companies of the Thirty-sixth Wisconsin Volunteer Infantry came up out of the Polegreen Branch Creek bottom, one hundred yards downhill and east of the church. For two days, they had enjoyed the refreshing clear waters of the two springs near the creek. At 240 strong, they climbed up the steep incline to the south of the creek and positioned themselves in earthworks at the edge of the woods where it fronted open farmland. As the Wisconsin soldiers looked across the field 225 yards southwest, they saw the Confederate earthworks. Behind these earthworks passing through Hundley's Corner on an east–west line were men of Breckinridge's division. From Hundley's Corner, the Confederate line ran parallel with Shady Grove Church Road for four hundred yards and then made a ninety-degree turn south toward the midpoint between Bethesda Church and Mechanicsville.

Breckinridge's people had the artillery support of the Powhatan Artillery (manning two twelve-pounder Napoleons and two rifled guns). Out in the field, there were Federal sharpshooters behind rifle pits, which had been dug by Confederate infantry but were overrun by Federals the day before. The troops in gray withheld their fire on the oncoming Federals until their targets were clearly identified and their aim sure. The first-person report of Charles Storke, who was in the Thirty-sixth Wisconsin Infantry and erected the monument near Hundley's Corner to honor his comrades, affirms that the order to fire came when the men in blue were as close as fifty yards. The historian of the Thirty-sixth Wisconsin wrote that the battle at Polegreen placed his regiment nearly at the head of the "Three Hundred Fighting Regiments" that suffered the highest casualties in the Civil War. He recorded that the dead, wounded and captured numbered 140. But Charles Storke, one of those captured, reported much higher casualties. He said, "Of the 240 men from the four companies of the 36th Wisconsin, 80 died immediately, 168 were wounded, and 39 were captured."

The Confederate battle line that ran through Hundley's Corner extended off to the northwest in an almost unbroken line for two miles. The action initiated by Gibbon on June 1 was centered on a front of 1,300 yards. That front was bisected by the Hanover Courthouse–Cold Harbor Road, which intersected the road at Hundley's Corner. The action described above covered the eastern half of the front from Hundley's Corner to the present Thirty-sixth Wisconsin monument. Beginning at Hundley's Corner and curving northwest, the Confederate works, after eight hundred yards, faced the front entrance of Polegreen Church, three hundred yards to the east. Farmlands lay between the earthworks and the church. As in the case of those fighting east of Hundley's Corner, the space between the Federal-occupied woods and the Confederate line was dotted with rifle pits that Confederates had built but Federals now occupied. William White noted in his diary:

On 1 June Kirkland's and Cooke's Brigades were desperately charged behind breastworks. The Forty-seventh was in splendid fighting trim on this occasion, and as the enemy started across an open field the order was given [to] us not to fire until a certain cannon fired, and company commanders were to order the fire by file. The Federal officers threw themselves in front of their men and most gallantly led them, but when the cannon sounded the signal, our deadly fire opened on them within fifty yards and it was so steady and accurate, for our men were perfectly cool, that before the companies had fired a round, the enemy was completely broken and routed, a large number of them killed and wounded. Our loss was almost nothing as the enemy, depending on giving us the bayonet, withheld their fire, until they were repulsed.

Amid the ebb and flow of events occurring along the front as the focus of the campaign shifted toward Old Cold Harbor, General Lee sent a dispatch to Secretary of War James Seddon, commending Kirkland's and Cooke's brigades. Meade had sent an order to Hancock to withdraw his corps after dark and to move, via Haw's Shop, to the rear of Bethesda Church. The intent was to get the Second Corps down to Old Cold Harbor in support of the Federal effort there. To carry out this order, Hancock directed the Second Division to withdraw first from the Totopotomoy by taking the direct road toward Haw's Shop. Barlow's First Division was to leave about the same time, go back up to Polly Hundley's Corner and return by the road down which it had advanced on May 29. Birney and his Third Division were to pull out last and follow Barlow's route. At Haw's Shop, all were to turn right on the Mechanicsville Road, cross the Totopotomoy and mass at the Via House, Grant's headquarters.

With the day's fighting over at Polegreen, the weary soldiers from the North withdrew, slung their knapsacks and left the Totopotomoy. They were expected by Grant to cover the distance to Cold Harbor, which was fifteen miles by the prescribed route, and be in the line of battle by daybreak the following day. As he was to discover, Grant underestimated the effort and time necessary to carry out his order, much to his sorrow.

Chapter 11

June 2, 1864

The Lull before the Storm

O n the afternoon of June 1, Grant ordered the Second Corps under Hancock to Cold Harbor, expecting to launch an all-out attack on a front extending from Old Cold Harbor to the Totopotomoy on the morning of June 2. At that time, he thought that Hancock would be positioned on the left flank of his line, Wright to Hancock's right, Smith in the center between Wright and Warren and Burnside up on the Totopotomoy near the Via House. However, Grant miscalculated the time necessary to get Hancock in position. By daybreak, he reassessed the situation and postponed the attack until late afternoon.

The Polegreen Confederates, having repulsed Gibbon's division, followed up their success by pressing after Hancock's corps as it withdrew. This went on all night. By daybreak, Heth's people confronted Burnside's right flank, anchored at the Whitlock House on the Totopotomoy. Upon reaching Haw's Shop before daylight, Hancock's corps turned right on the road to Mechanicsville. This was the road down which Warren had marched on the twenty-ninth after he crossed the Pamunkey at Hanovertown. Hancock's line of march had him passing down the road to Bethesda Church, about two miles in the rear of Burnside's line. From Bethesda Church, the Second Corps marched to the rear of Warren, Smith and Wright and took position to Wright's left and rear. Hancock's report to Humphreys at Meade's headquarters underscores why his men were not ready for action:

The First Division of my corps (Barlow's) arrived here at 6 o'clock, and is now forming in rear of General Wright's left. It will be some time before the corps is up and in position, having been considerably opened out during the night. On consultation with General Wright I think I shall form on his left. He thinks that two divisions should reach to the high ground, virtually controlling the ground between it and the Chickahominy. I shall admit no unnecessary delay, but it will be several hours before my command is ready to attack. I have about twelve regiments on picket, who did not leave till this morning, and there was a good deal of straggling, owing to extreme fatigue of the men and the dusty roads.

Hancock had been further hindered when ordered to leave Birney's division with Baldy Smith's Eighteenth Corps because Smith's people lacked ammunition and supplies. By 2:00 p.m., it was apparent to Grant that his army was not going to be in position for an attack on Lee by that evening. At 1:30 p.m., Grant had ordered the attack for 5:00 p.m., but a half hour later, he rescinded the order and postponed the attack until 4:30 the next morning, June 3.

After the Federal demonstration at Polegreen and the subsequent withdrawal of Hancock's corps on the night of the first, Breckinridge was ordered to withdraw from Hundley's Corner and march to the right at Turkey Hill. This would place him again in front of Hancock, both commands having moved simultaneously to the southeast almost seven miles. Hancock and Breckinridge left the Polegreen area at 10:00 p.m. on the first, but the Confederates had a guide who misdirected them and had made it only to Mechanicsville (four miles away) by breakfast time the next morning.

To shorten his lines and mass his troops preparatory to his planned all-out attack, Grant ordered a redeployment of some of his troops at 7:30 a.m. During the previous forty-eight hours, Warren's corps was strung out on a five-mile front from Shady Grove Church Road near the Thirty-sixth Wisconsin monument, past Bethesda Church and within a mile of Wooddy's farm on the Old Cold Harbor Road. All his regiments were at the front—there were no reserves. Since crossing the Pamunkey on May 29 at Hanovertown, Burnside's corps had been the least involved in combat of the Army of the Potomac's four infantry corps. With the withdrawal of Hancock in support of Grant's plan to concentrate his force on a shorter front, Burnside was ordered into position on Warren's right at Bethesda Church. Along with Warren, Burnside would guard the Union right against a Confederate flank attack.

By daylight, Heth, joined by Rodes and Gordon of Early's corps, had pushed his men up to Burnside's right, and lively skirmishing ensued. When Burnside received orders to position his corps in echelon to Warren's right, he was reluctant to do so, and Meade repeated the orders twice. The following evening, communication from Meade to Grant set forth the strategy for the 4:30 a.m. June 3 attack and also indicates a sensitive command problem within the high command of the Army of the Potomac that had to be dealt with:

> GENERAL: *I send Major* [Washington A.] *Roebling, of Warren's staff, who will explain the position of affairs on the right when he left. It would appear from Major Roebling's statement that the enemy at dark were in force in front of both Burnside and Warren. I do not believe they will remain in front of Burnside. I have, however, sent orders both to Warren and Burnside that they must, at all hazards, attack the enemy to-morrow at 4:30 a.m., and if he is not in force in their front they must swing round to the left and follow up and attack on Smith's right flank. In like manner, should the enemy be in great force in their front and check them, then our attacks here ought to prevail, and we will swing by the right and move up on Warren's left. In order to ensure energy and harmony of action, I propose to place, with your approval, Burnside under Warren's orders.*

Burnside harbored resentment toward Meade, whom he had once ranked and yet from whom he had to take orders. Meade's suggestion that Burnside be placed under Warren prompted Grant to question the propriety of this arrangement. Grant responded to Meade by saying, "I do not know whether it would be right to place Burnside under Warren, the latter being his junior, but I would direct him to advise with Warren, and to act in concert with him." There were other communications to both Warren and Burnside that day, urging them to cooperate.

In postponing the attack until June 3, Grant directed that the corps commanders let their men rest in preparation for the next day's battle. He also called for only defensive action, except that "commanders should have their lines in a defensible condition and sufficiently closed to the enemy. Division commanders will examine the ground well and have the proper points of attack selected. It is very probable that an assault will be ordered at the earliest hour to-morrow. This will be regarded as confidential among the division commanders." This was reflected in Hancock's orders to his division commanders.

Earlier, Grant had entertained the idea of anchoring his left on the Chickahominy, holding Grapevine Bridge and crossing to the south side of the river. From these crossings, he saw the opportunity to get between Lee and Richmond. Except for a brief excursion to the Chickahominy by Sheridan's cavalry, the closest the Army of the Potomac got was the position held by Barlow of Hancock's corps, more than a mile from the river.

The decision by Grant to postpone the attack until June 3 contributed to the last great victory by the Army of Northern Virginia. It provided extra time for Lee to redeploy three divisions from his left to his right and into a position where they could fortify the ground and be most effective.

It was clear by daylight on the second that none of Hancock's men remained on the Totopotomoy. It was time for Mahone and Wilcox of Hill's corps to get down to Cold Harbor as soon as possible. By 3:00 p.m., both had arrived on the right of the Confederate line. Wilcox filled in a gap between Breckinridge and Hoke, also providing some reserves for Heth. Mahone came up in support of Breckinridge, and men from both units drove the enemy from Turkey Hill. Following this action, Lee moved Wilcox to the right of Breckinridge and closer to the Chickahominy.

Of equal importance, the delay provided every Confederate soldier in the line time to dig into the sandy soil of eastern Hanover County with whatever implement was at hand. Few had shovels, but tin cups, spoons, bayonets, canteen halves, sticks and bare hands were employed. When possible, trees were felled and abatis formed, behind which men took careful aim.

For the Union army, the second day of June was one of some respite from the shooting, though not entirely. The Confederate sharpshooting continued throughout the day. Some Union soldiers who had overrun the first skirmish line of the Confederates were pinned down all day by the steady rain of Minié balls and frequent artillery shot. Though spared the danger of an order to attack the gray line, it was still too great a hazard to attempt a withdrawal to safer positions. The count of Union casualties resulting from the action on June 1 was delayed until daybreak on the second and indicated at least one thousand men of the Eighteenth Corps had been killed or wounded. The Thirteenth New Hampshire, among other regiments, was so badly mauled that it could not participate in the attack on June 3. A diarist of this unit described the scene that met his eyes early on the morning of the second:

> *An errand early to-day took the writer about half a mile through the woods to the left, and a more terrible picture of war can scarcely be imagined. The*

dead are lying everywhere. The bodies show but little evidence of suffering, but the limbs are stretched out stiff and at almost every possible angle. Many bodies are bent backwards, as if the spine were trying to touch ends that way. One body is thus arched up, and is resting upon the shoulders and heels. The coat-capes are turned up over many faces, other faces are bare, others hidden, the bodies lying face down; but the most lie as they fell, and are badly torn—it is a walk of sickening and unutterable horrors. Along the line of a fence, near the ridge, or crest of the bluff over which we charged, one could walk several rods upon the bodies almost covering the ground, lying in every conceivable position, and piled one upon another. Among these are some sitting bolt upright, gun in hand, in a posture almost as natural as life, and appearing as if they had not moved a muscle after being shot. One lies attentively examining the lock of his musket, his head to the foe, and a bullet hole through the lower part of his face. Many bodies of horses, too, are lying among the men.

The scene of our charge presents this morning a strange sight. A man a little apart by himself on the crest, but one of the skirmish line through which we advanced to the charge, had his gun about half way between the position of "ready" and "aim," when he was instantly killed: and there he is this morning, scarcely changed in position, but resting quite firmly and naturally on one knee, his left shoulder against a stump, while he holds his gun raised and cocked, his head leaning a little to one side, peering around the stump as if about to find a good mark among the enemy and to shoot. Those who have occasion to pass in front of his gun, before he is removed, instinctively start, and step quickly out of line of the aim of the dead man's gun. It does not seem possible that any man when dead could retain a position so life-like. But this is not the only case of similar fixed rigidity of muscles after instant death.

The field of our charge bears a little to the right this morning, and contains many bodies of the Union dead lying in full view. The 13th are so badly cut up, that they are not called upon for much duty to-day; are ordered to preserve silence, not to fire a shot, and to remain hidden under the ridge or crest and the trees as much as possible, and avoid betraying their position.

The Army of Northern Virginia had now been engaged, almost daily, in combat for a month. In the two years that Lee had been in command of the army, there had never been a campaign or engagement that had lasted this long. The toll on both sides had been heavy. Losses on the Northern side were rapidly approaching the equivalent of the entire Southern force facing them. The worst was yet to come.

As the nearly exhausted men on both sides prepared for the inevitable next battle, their thoughts were tempered by the visions of comrades wounded and dying, by the scenes of shattered bodies and the unburied dead and the cries of the wounded. There was also the painful reality that many would die without anyone knowing who they were or from where they came. Added to the obvious horrors of war was the realization that many would never return to their homes and that even when the war was over, their loved ones would have no way of identifying their remains, should there be any. Unless the individual soldier carried on his body or his clothing some identification, there was no way to identify him. (It was not until 1901 that the government began supplying the dog tags so familiar to soldiers in the twentieth century.) This identification might take the form of a small metal coin, which was inscribed with the soldier's name and military unit, that was hung on a chain and worn around the neck. The second most preferred ID was a decorative pin against the background of a cross or some other patriotic symbol. On this also would be the soldier's name and military unit. Both of these items would have been purchased from sutler stores, which were owned by civilians who traveled with the army. The very poor soldier might be unable to afford an identification tag. Perhaps it was ominous that, on the night of the second, some Union soldiers were seen writing their names on pieces of paper and pinning them in the seams of their uniforms, in order that their bodies could be identified. One soldier wrote in his diary: "June 3. Cold Harbor. I was killed."

Chapter 12

June 3, 1864

A t 4:30 a.m., Hades erupted at Cold Harbor. Nine miles away in Richmond, a sound was heard that had never been equaled in the history of the city. In 1862, the Army of the Potomac had advanced to Seven Pines, about nine miles east of the center of the city. McClellan had brought his troops up the peninsula as the Confederates withdrew from Yorktown and Williamsburg to defend their capital city. The overly cautious and hesitant Union general never launched an all-out assault on Richmond, but that was two years ago. Now it was a different story. The present commander, U.S. Grant, had been pounding away at the Army of Northern Virginia for a month, all the way from the Rapidan crossings to Cold Harbor, in an attempt to make a breakthrough, destroy the Army of Northern Virginia and capture the same prize. He had no intention of being denied, and he was determined, at almost any cost, to humble Lee and the men in tattered gray and march victoriously into the enemy's capital. This early Friday morning attack was launched with a thunderous artillery barrage that shook Richmond to consciousness in the rudest fashion.

Though the citizens in the city began the day with the surprise awakening, their defenders in the field in Hanover County from Polegreen to Cold Harbor were not in the least caught off guard. Every possible preparation had been made for the general assault that Grant had ordered. The Southerners had been provided ample time and more to entrench themselves in the sandy soil of eastern Hanover County. Where there was any advantage to be gained, each regiment and each soldier had seized it during the forty-eight hours prior to the Union attack. Shallow earthworks were deepened, trees were felled to provide abatis and traverses running from the main defense line to secondary lines were dug to provide a route of withdrawal, should the oncoming hordes threaten to overrun the first line. Insofar as it was at all possible, both the artillery and the infantry units sought the highpoints of the rolling land to position themselves for minimum exposure to shot and shell from an opponent that enjoyed superiority of numbers in all categories.

At the moment the attack was launched, the sun had not yet risen. The blackness of the night was just beginning to give way to enough grayness for the human eye to make distinctions on the ground level. While Grant had issued a general order that called for an attack by all five corps of the Union army, Warren's Fifth Corps and Burnside's Ninth participated very little. Opposing these two fully equipped and manned units were only Early's corps and Heth's division from A.P. Hill's corps. The brunt of the Union assault at Cold Harbor was assumed by the corps of Hancock, Wright and Smith. The defenders of Richmond opposing them were principally divisions of Hill's corps, Anderson's corps and the divisions of Breckinridge and Hoke. Within minutes, the artillery cannonade was followed by the charge of the infantry. The withering fire of the Confederates took a horrible toll on the advancing frontal attack. Wave after wave moved across open fields and up gentle slopes until the ground was littered with the dead and wounded, and still they came. Repeatedly the command to charge was given until, after thirty minutes, the response to the order had diminished to no more than rifle-muskets discharging into the air in the hands of men lying on the ground, refusing to expose their bodies to certain death. Casualty reports for the morning ranged from 5,000 to 7,000 thousand for the Union army and around 1,300 for the Confederates. By five o'clock in the morning, the outcome had been decided. Few, if any, units ventured into the field the rest of the day, though firing continued from concealed positions until Grant ordered cessation at one o'clock in the afternoon along the entire front. It was the last major victory in the field for Lee and the Army of Northern Virginia. It was considered by many to be the worst defeat in the field for Grant. In his memoirs written years after the war, he acknowledged his regret at having issued the orders for the last assaults at Cold Harbor.

The great loss in killed, wounded and captured men on the morning of June 3, in the eyes of many, including a noticeable number of Grant's own men, was not just the high cost of the attempt to overrun the Confederate positions on Friday morning. Grant's behavior during the next three days fueled a disgust in many of his soldiers that lasted long after the war was

Collecting remains of those killed at Cold Harbor for reinternment. Cold Harbor, Virginia. *Courtesy of Wikimedia Commons.*

over. The Union commander's refusal to admit failure and ask for a truce to remove his dead and wounded from the field of battle was paid for by the death of many wounded who might have been saved. For the dead on the field, it did not matter. To their friends and families who later learned of the horrors at Cold Harbor, the indignities that accompanied men's bodies, which rotted away under the hot summer sun, were heartbreaking. But the cries for help that came from the lips of the wounded, some of which went on for more than three days unanswered, was a tragedy that could have been averted in a fratricidal war that was shameful enough without this type of aggravation. After several ambiguous communications from Grant to Lee, the Union commander finally, at the end of the beginning of the fourth day following the initial assault, followed the normal and accepted military procedure and asked Lee for a truce to clear the battlefield of his dead and wounded. There was never any need for Lee to make such a request, since his men had occupied defensive positions during the entire attack and had no need to venture onto the field of conflict. The Confederate casualties generated by the Union offensive had occurred within the lines of the Southerners and were managed without any reason to obtain the counsel or approval of the Union command.

The citizens of Richmond were elated but not surprised to learn of the Confederate victory at Cold Harbor. Their confidence in Lee and his men had been unshaken for two years, and the reports that came into the city in the afternoon and evening of June 3 were another confirmation of their trust. But the wiser heads in the capital city knew that with every battle the army diminished in size, while seemingly inexhaustible replacements were available to the enemy.

June 3, 1864, was one of the worst days of the four-year war. The spring campaign that began at the crossings of the Rapidan a month earlier was now, for all practical purposes, ended. Grant had been confident at the beginning that he would, by sheer numbers and brute force, smash the Army of Northern Virginia, which some of his subordinate commanders held in contempt. Now at the end of the monthlong effort, and with his own casualties exceeding the entire strength of the Army of Northern Virginia, he had not produced the victory about which he had felt so confident and had boasted of doing. The Union commander, who had notified Washington on May 26 that Lee's army was whipped, now ate his words and tasted the bitterness of failure. For several days following the disastrous assaults on this Friday morning, there was sporadic firing by both armies, but no effort was made to occupy the lines of the opposition. Lee dispatched Breckinridge to Lynchburg four days after the fierce fighting on the third to help stop the Union attacks under Major General David "Black Dave" Hunter and hinder his advance eastward with his army of twenty thousand. Heth, who had held off the attack at Polegreen on June 1 and who had been pressing Burnside's Ninth Corps on Grant's right flank, was brought down to the Confederate right and held in reserve where Breckinridge had fought. Grant moved Burnside from the extreme right and placed him at a right angle to the main Union line near Beulah Church, where he entrenched to defend against any effort by the Confederates to make a move on Smith's Eighteenth Corps.

Increasing pressure on the Southerners generated by Hunter in the west prompted Lee to take a significant risk and withdraw Early's corps from the Bethesda Church segment of the Cold Harbor line and dispatch it to the west on the morning of June 13. By a rather incredible coincidence, Lee received word at the same hour of Early's departure that the Union line had been evacuated during the previous night. Grant was headed toward the James River and to the eventual ten-month Siege of Petersburg.

The war that many thought would be over within a matter of weeks, or at most months, had entered its final year, and a price had been paid that neither side could have imagined. Almost half the major battles of the war fought during the four years took place in Virginia. Consequently, the casualties of dead, wounded and captured that accompanied those battles were larger in Virginia than any other state, Northern or Southern. What is often overlooked by students and others interested in the Civil War is that Virginia was the state that experienced the greatest loss in personal property and the only state to suffer the permanent loss of territory. The suffering of the civilian population continued long after the war had ended. Cities like Petersburg and Richmond suffered enormous destruction.

In a state that saw more fighting than any other, a disproportionate amount of that action occurred in the three counties that surrounded the capital of the Confederacy—Hanover, Henrico and Chesterfield. Of these three, Hanover experienced the most as two major campaigns moved through its land, leaving in their wakes death and destruction. The war also left a legacy of civilian pain and loss that spared hardly a family or individual within the bounds of these counties. Now on June 13, 1864, the worst was over for Hanover. Grant and the Army of the Potomac slipped away during the night and were headed for the south side of the James River. Concerned that the Union army might still make another effort to enter Richmond from the east, Lee moved his army across the Chickahominy in his continuing defense of the city.

The scarred land that had been the scene of the struggle for religious and civil liberty during the days of Samuel Davies and that had produced the orator of the American Revolution Patrick Henry now awaited the end of the War Between the States. The end would come ten months down the road, but even then, veterans of the war returned home to begin a new struggle—to survive amid the trail of destruction left in the path of armies.

Chapter 13

Day's End at Cold Harbor

The major fighting near the Totopotomoy on June 3 was over by 6:00 p.m. At Cold Harbor, the worst was just beginning. The abortive Confederate attack had occurred shortly after daybreak in the vicinity of Beulah Church. Since Wright's Sixth Corps did not begin to arrive until 9:00 a.m., the Union force must have been under the command of Sheridan. After Keitt was struck down, Kershaw's division withdrew to a position parallel to and about one hundred yards west of the Wooddy farm on the Old Cold Harbor–Bethesda Church Road (Route 633).

When the Sixth Corps arrived at Old Cold Harbor crossroads via Old Church in midmorning, they fanned out a half mile west on the road to New Cold Harbor (Route 156). At this point, the corps was placed in position to the right and left of the road, forming a front before Anderson and Hoke, who had moved to Anderson's right toward Turkey Hill. Wright's men extended about a half mile north of the Cold Harbor Road, parallel to the Old Cold Harbor–Bethesda Church Road.

When Smith's men (the reinforced Eighteenth Corps) arrived at Old Cold Harbor crossroads, they were ordered into position on the right of the Sixth Corps. To reach that area, they took the road to Beulah Church and through the fields to the left and right of the road. The arriving troops, covered with dust and nearly exhausted, passed through the open farm strewn with the debris of battle left from the Confederate morning attack on Sheridan. As the Thirteenth New Hampshire regiment was brought up to hold the right flank of the Eighteenth Corps, the scene was terrible. Captain James M. Durell reported what he saw:

> *Near one o'clock p.m. we enter the Army of the Potomac in action, and pass over a portion of the field, near the right of the 18th Corps line, where the irregular fighting has already swept. Trees are broken, torn off blown in pieces, and the ground torn up, by shells, fragments of which strew the ground; while the bullet marks appear everywhere and on everything, beyond numbering or estimating. The dead are lying all about us, chiefly rebel dead; and the wounded Union soldiers are coming back from the front in great numbers, many of them borne on stretchers, or assisted by other men. One General [Colonel Keitt] among the number. We cross a wide, open field, and halt among some of the little oak-trees. Here are quite a number of the rebel dead, and a pile of their knapsacks. One C.S.A. knapsack here, being vigorously kicked, yields to the writer a new, blue and gold, pocket edition of Scott's Lady of the Lake, that is afterwards read by many, and read aloud for the entertainment of many more, in the Cold Harbor trenches. The men of the thirteenth at this little halt among the oaks commence to lunch, but are moved on before they can finish. We now pass through large bodies of waiting troops of the 6th Corps, who look us over curiously, and several batteries of artillery; a few rebel prisoners pass us going toward the rear, all smiling and jocular, with the air of men just relieved from duty; mounted horsemen are flying in every direction and at the top of their horses' speed—and the care with which a swiftly running horse will avoid stepping on the body of a man lying on the ground is truly marvelous. On the way we file around the burning ruins of a building, said to be Beulah church, near D. Wooddy's, on the Bethesda church road.*

No all-out attack from either army occurred throughout the day, until the Eighteenth Corps finally arrived and was in position. Smith's men took their position to the right of the Sixth Corps and extended north just beyond Beulah Church. One division (Martindale's) was held in reserve behind the right wing of the northernmost Eighteenth Corps.

A ravine about three-fourths of a mile long extends from the Cold Harbor Road north toward Beulah Church. This formed the initial dividing line between the two armies. The western side of the ravine rises more steeply than the eastern. On the rim of the western side, the Confederates established their first line of rifle pits. Three hundred yards behind those were the trenches supported by Anderson's artillery.

View of the battlefield at Cold Harbor, Virginia.
Courtesy of Wikimedia Commons.

At 6:00 p.m., the twenty-five-thousand-man assault was launched by half of the Sixth Corps and the men of the Eighteenth along a one-mile front from the Old Cold Harbor–New Cold Harbor Road (Route 156) north to the Wooddy farm and Beulah Church ruins. The attack advanced from east to west down a slight grade, across the ravine, partly through a shallow pond and up a steep grade forty feet in height to the first skirmish line of the Confederates. The fire from the men in gray took a heavy toll. The Thirteenth New Hampshire had the honor of occupying the northernmost position on this first day of heavy fighting at Cold Harbor. A gap of one mile remained between the right of Smith's troops and the left of Warren's.

As the men in blue advanced from the vicinity of the Wooddy House, they passed by the pond (the only one in the area and still exists) and saw a strange sight: "Quite a number of Union soldiers, standing and lying, half sunk in the mud and water of the pond—dead; all having been shot while attempting to cross to the skirmish line, before the 13th came up."

The battle that began at 6:00 p.m. continued for three and half hours. The forces of Wright and Smith penetrated the first line of defense of Anderson, occupying the rifle pits and taking five hundred prisoners. Counterattacking Confederates tempered the initial success of the Federals, recovering some of their lines and, for the most part, maintaining their defensive position, all the time digging deeper and more formidable earthworks. Meade foresaw that possibility, and at 10:00 p.m., he sent a dispatch to Wright seeking advice:

Where had I better direct Hancock to go? I should think on your left, or would it not be better he should support you in another attack? I do not like extending too much. It is the trouble we have had all day long of occupying too long lines and not massing enough…I think we ought to attack as early as possible in the morning—Smith, yourself, and Hancock; Warren also.

If we give them any time, they will dig so as to prevent any advance on our part.

The number of Confederates engaged near Old Cold Harbor on June 1 was a little more than half that of June 3, and the number of assaults ordered by Grant was a fraction of those on the third; yet the casualties were significant. Union field hospitals reported that 1,800 wounded were brought in from the Sixth and Eighteenth Corps. In the battle lines, men reported hundreds killed. Under the date of June 3, Charles W. Washburn of Company G, a member of the Thirteenth's Band and temporarily employed at the hospital, wrote:

Thousands were wounded [on] *June 1st. We had poor accommodations. The wounded were brought back to the rear, a mile or so, on stretchers, and laid on the ground in a field, and we put up bushes, the next day, to keep the sun off a little. The Surgeons worked night and day, cutting off legs and arms, and extracting bullets and pieces of shells, from every part of men's bodies. All had to lie on the ground, both before and after the operations upon them. It rained the night of June 2nd, and many of the wounded had little cover and some of them no cover at all.*

General Gibbon had observed early in the 1864 campaign that if either army got as much as an eight-hour head start on the other side in digging earthworks, it was nearly impossible to dislodge them. Here at Cold Harbor, Anderson and Hoke, who bore the brunt of the fateful attack of the Union army, had at least fifty hours to prepare their defense. While Lee had not realized the victory for which he hoped by his early morning attack on this day, Grant's miscalculating the time necessary to move Wright down from the Totopotomoy, plus his mistake in sending Smith's corps to New Castle, created a situation that boded ill for his forces at Cold Harbor.

Addenda

A Tale of Two Soldiers and Polegreen Church

The First: A Confederate Cannoneer

In the course of preparing the necessary papers nominating the Polegreen Church site for a place on the Register of Historic Landmarks in Virginia and subsequently to the National Register of Historic Places, it seemed desirable and important to document the destruction of the church on June 1, 1864. Initially, the assumption was that the building was set on fire by shellfire from the Union army since at this time in the war, it was not likely that church buildings in open country would be torched by Southern soldiers fighting in their homeland. My efforts went on for months in attempting to reconstruct the events of the battle around Polegreen Church on its final day. In particular, the search was on for an eyewitness account of the burning of the church.

During the time of the centennial recognition of the Civil War, Edwin Bearss, future chief historian of the National Park Service, was tasked with preparing a series of sixteen maps covering the Battle of Cold Harbor from May 30 to June 13. The focus of the maps was on the action at Cold Harbor; hence, the areas northwest covering Totopotomoy Creek and Polegreen Church were not portrayed. In fact, the northern border of Bearss's maps cut through Hundley's Corner, which is three-tenths of a mile south of the

Polegreen Church site. Yet Bearss noted one critical piece of information that came close to being "off the map." That was the location of Hardaway's Artillery Battery. With that lead, the research I conducted over a period of months led me to the archives of the Virginia Historical Society. Hardaway's battalion contained the Third Company of the Richmond Howitzers. On June 4, 1864, Edward S. McCarthy, beloved captain of a battery of the First Company of the Richmond Howitzers, was killed at Cold Harbor. In 1883, his brother, Carlton McCarthy, published a history of the Richmond Howitzers, and the segment dealing with the Third Company was composed of the diary of Sergeant William S. White. I realized that the discovery of the coveted eyewitness account of the burning of Polegreen Church on June 2, 1864, was close at hand. Turning quickly to the date of June 2, 1864, in White's diary was one of those exciting moments that researchers dream about. In bold type were the words "Attempt to Force Our Lines at Polegreen Church, Wednesday, June 1st [sic]." Three paragraphs on, White, the young Confederate cannoneer born in Hanover County four miles from Polegreen, wrote, as reported in this volume relating to the action of June 2, that it was a shot from his gun that set the church afire. The shelling was done in an attempt to dislodge Federal sharpshooters who were using it for cover. No effort was ever made to rebuild one of the most historic and significant of all dissenter churches in colonial Virginia. The site of the church was virtually abandoned, the congregation being too poor to rebuild. In time, trees grew where the building had stood, and the neglected cemetery was vandalized and robbed of most of its monuments.

For 125 years, there seemed to be no special need to know what the old church looked like. But in 1989, the Presbytery of Hanover, which had been founded at Polegreen in 1755, obtained legal title to the historic site. The presbytery turned to me and directed that some appropriate memorial be established on the site to the work of Samuel Davies and the Hanover dissenters. Since 1989, interest has increased in interpreting this important chapter in colonial American history. The site was nominated to the National Register of Historic Places for its significance in the categories of religion, archaeology, architecture and military.

The understandable outgrowth of interest and research in this place has resulted in a quest to know as nearly as possible what the building was like. At hand were a few written descriptions of the structure. The oldest was a simple three-sentence comment of a minister who visited the site in 1790. He described it as follows:

The church in which he [Davies] *preached in Hanover, and which was erected for him in 1757, is still standing. It is about ten miles from the city of Richmond, and is a remarkably plain building, of wood, without a steeple, and capable of accommodating about five hundred persons. In pleasant weather, the number of persons who came to hear him was so great, that the church could not contain them, and worship was held in a neighboring grove.*

The work done in 1989–90 by the Department of Archaeology of Virginia Commonwealth University revealed a major portion of the brick foundation of the church. Nothing of the building had been visible above the ground. The discovery of the foundation was very important to the process of nomination to the National Register of Historic Places. While that honor has been achieved, there still remained no visual image of what stood on that foundation. This was obviously highly desirable. A photo by Matthew Brady's men or those of Sullivan would be a dream come true. But so far, none has been forthcoming.

Of the two tantalizing questions—"Did anyone who saw Polegreen's destruction leave a written account of it?" and "What did the church really look like before it burned?"—one had been answered. A Confederate soldier, trying to dislodge Federal sharpshooters, had fired his Napoleon artillery piece at the building, set it afire and left a dramatic account of his thoughts as he watched it burn. As 1992 came to a close, the second question was yet unanswered, but behind the scenes, things were happening to change all that—and almost unbelievably, a Union soldier was the key.

The Other: A Union Engineer

The sequence of events leading to the discovery of a visual likeness of the historic Polegreen Church is somewhat remarkable—that is, if one considers the mathematical odds against the series of events occurring that led to its discovery. Or it is at least remarkable if one identifies with those responsible for and committed to interpreting the history of this important eighteenth-century site. The contemporary incidents that bear directly on this part of our story begin with a near disaster at the Manasses battlefield in 1991. Front-page news stories in many daily papers told of plans to develop a large shopping mall close to vital portions of that national landmark. The uproar that followed resulted in Congress appropriating in excess of $130 million to purchase the land from the developer. The debate surrounding the decision served as a wake-up call to many, legislators and others, that a number of important Civil War battlefield sites were already lost or seriously threatened. The same Congress that bought back Manasses also created the Civil War Sites Advisory Commission, charged with identifying the most important battle sites and their threatened states.

To carry out the responsibilities given it, the Civil War Sites Advisory Commission held a number of public hearings to receive input from all persons interested in this problem. One of these hearings was held in Richmond, Virginia, an area that contains a disproportionately large number of important battlefield sites. I was encouraged by friends interested in preservation to address the commission on the urgency of the need for help in central Virginia in particular. I was introduced to the commission as the president of the Historic Polegreen Church Foundation. Unbeknownst to me, there was a magazine writer who was developing a story on the threatened loss of important Civil War sites in Virginia in the audience. Unbeknownst to the magazine writer was the role he was playing in the discovery of the needed visual representation of Polegreen Church. Even more interesting was that it was a mistake in his story that proved to be of significance in the ultimate solution to this quest. Five months later, on a Saturday morning in January 1993, the phone rang in Richmond.

"Is this the home of the rector of the Polegreen Church?" asked the caller.

"This is the home of Bob Bluford, but the Polegreen Church was burned down during the Civil War."

"My name is Barbara Ferguson, and I live in Virginia Beach. I have just read an article in the *Mid-Atlantic Country* magazine that quoted Reverend Bluford as having spoken about Civil War battlefield preservation, and the writer of the story identified him as being the pastor of the Polegreen Church. Members of my family and I have been trying to find out for the past fifteen years where the Polegreen Church is located. My grandfather was an engineer in General McClellan's army in 1862, and some of his military papers, including an artist sketchpad, were found in 1978 in a basement in Philadelphia. The words 'Polegreen Church' were written on three sketches, but no state or county was mentioned. When I read this magazine article, the name 'Polegreen' leaped off the page. Would you like to see the sketches?"

What had seemed a virtual impossibility for three years now seemed altogether possible.

Those of us working on the Polegreen project had assumed that there might have been a photograph or a sketch in some Hanover County attic, all nearby libraries and archives having been searched. No one could have guessed that a Union soldier from New York and his descendants in Philadelphia were the custodians of the information so much desired and needed in Hanover County and Richmond, Virginia, 131 years after he had been on the Polegreen site.

During the spring of 1862, the Army of the Potomac under General George B. McClellan advanced up the lower peninsula in Virginia with the intention of taking the capital of the Confederacy. The armies of the North and South, particularly during the first two years of the war, were seriously hampered by the lack of accurate maps of the ground over which troops were moved and on which battles were fought. This was certainly true during the Peninsula Campaign. As McClellan moved up toward Richmond in May 1862, he expected he might launch attacks directly from the east of the city and from the northeast through Hanover County. In order to plan an attack, particularly through Hanover County, it would be necessary to have some semblance of maps. To accomplish this, he ordered Brigadier General Daniel P. Woodbury and members of the Fiftieth New York Volunteer Engineers to enter the southeastern end of Hanover and map it and portions of Henrico County, of which Richmond was the county seat.

Among the New York volunteers was a nineteen-year-old soldier by the name of Lieutenant Thomas W. Farrell. Farrell and his companions made their way up from Yorktown by boat, and at West Point, they entered the left stream and continued up the Pamunkey River. At White House Landing in New Kent County, they disembarked and headed for Old Church in eastern Hanover. Farrell was not only an engineer trained in mapmaking but also an artist, and he carried with him an artist sketchpad. The pad in which the Polegreen sketches were found was three by five inches. Farrell had sketched a Union camp scene at Yorktown, as well as an interior sketch of St. Peter's Episcopal Church in northwest New Kent County, as he journeyed toward Hanover.

On May 29, 1862, Farrell was at the Polegreen site. It is possible that he camped there, as there was a spring nearby that had served the church members for over a century. Union soldiers in the 1864 campaign that carried them through Polegreen commented on their use of the spring. Here on the site, Farrell sketched the church from his view of its southern exposure. He then entered the building and sketched the interior looking toward the east from its west-end entrance—this is looking toward the pulpit. He then propped open the front door with a chair, walked down the center aisle and sketched the interior looking westward. On the borders of the two interior sketches are drawn several enlarged details of such items as post capitals and scrolled ends of pews.

Through the courtesy of Norman Albright, Farrell's great-grandson in Bromall, Pennsylvania, copies of the three sketches were sent to the Historic Polegreen Church Foundation. Albright and his father discovered three paper shopping bags filled with Farrell's military records, papers and his sketchpad as they were cleaning out Farrell's home to sell it. The sketches were taken to the architectural staff of the Colonial Williamsburg Foundation, consultants on the Polegreen project, for their observation and study. Upon viewing the three drawings, the reactions of the research architects present were expressed in the words of the recently retired vice-president of education, Dr. Robert Birney: "This is astonishing, that first-generation material such as these sketches have come to light just when you need it."

The tale of two soldiers and Polegreen Church can be summed up simply: It was a Confederate soldier who was forced to fire the shot that lamentably destroyed Polegreen, and it was a Union soldier's artistic interest in the church that left us the precious visual legacy of its existence.

THE FOURTH GUN

Third Company, Richmond Howitzers

War can be an occasion that produces unusual expressions of camaraderie. Men who might have never selected particular individuals as friends under normal circumstances have created strong bonds of devotion and attachment when sharing the stress of mortal combat. Since war is not an entirely rational endeavor, it should not be a surprise that men not uncommonly develop emotional attachments to inanimate objects such as weapons, ships, tanks, planes and other pieces of combat equipment. The Civil War produced similar experiences. The fourth gun of the Third Company of the Richmond Howitzers, the one that leveled Polegreen Church, became the object of devotion of some who manned and cared for it during the many engagements in which it was involved.

William S. White, during the first year and a half of the war, had commanded a variety of artillery pieces as the fourth gunner of his company. The first piece assigned to him was a brass howitzer, and by the time he obtained his Napoleon on November 2, 1863, he had directed artillery fire of Dahlgren howitzers, Parrott rifled guns and three-inch steel rifled guns. Some of the pieces he used had been captured either in battle or by Confederate raids on Union supply columns or depots. Five days after White's detachment was issued its "splendid Napoleon" on November 2, 1863, his company was ordered out of their camp at Mitchell's Station to Kelly's Ford, ten miles from Culpeper. He described the effort to carry out the order and the near loss of the fourth gun as follows:

> *Twas pretty severe on us, to quit our nice little huts that we had just finished, and go out without shelter, but such is the fate of the soldier and we submitted cheerfully.*
>
> *Left our camp a little before sundown, marching in the direction of Culpeper [sic] Courthouse until within two miles of that place when we took the road to Stephensburg, and then to Kelley's Ford. It was a dark, cold night and marching over very rough roads, we made but slow progress. My gun getting behind the battalion, the horses being unable to keep up, we were left to get along as best we could. On getting within two or three miles of Kelley's Ford, our battalion was ordered back to Brandy Station, and, being without support, was compelled to make a long circuitous march by Stephensburg, instead of taking the direct road.*
>
> *Finally, the horses to my gun came to a dead halt, and refused to move an inch farther—they were completely broken down. The battalion had moved on—'twas dark as Erebus and I was left all alone in my glory, commanding a splendid Napoleon, with six broken down horses, and scarcely a single cannonier with me. More also, the enemy's line was but a short distance from us and an advance was hourly expected. I sent one of the drivers on to report to Lieutenant Paine, commanding our company, and to ask for more horses, as it was impossible to move farther.*
>
> *What next to be done? Taking matters coolly, I lay down to await results, but ere long the tramp of soldiery aroused me from my nap, and I found they were our advanced pickets at [Kelley's] Ford, the enemy having crossed the river and driven them off.*
>
> *Some one [sic] calls out—"What gun is that?"*
>
> *"Fourth gun, Third Howitzers."*
>
> *"Didn't we fight with you'n's at Chancellorsville?"*
>
> *"What command do you belong to?"*
>
> *"Rode's [sic] men—Alabamians."*
>
> *"Yes, you did."*
>
> *"Fall in, boys, we can't lose that gun."*
>
> *And those brave Alabamians, some with their great strong shoulders against the wheels, and some leading, encouraging and whipping up*

the jaded and broken down horses, "whooped things up," until we were completely out of danger.

It was in the early days of the spring campaign of 1864 that the men of the Third Company had an unforgettable scare. For a brief time, their position on May 10, in line near Spotsylvania Courthouse, was overrun by Union infantry and all four of their guns captured. White's diary account tells how, for a time, he and other companions of the Richmond Howitzers found themselves fighting as infantrymen before recovering their artillery pieces. He wrote candidly of his humiliation at seeing some Confederate soldiers surrendering without firing a shot. He described May 10, 1864, as one of the darkest days of the Third Company. The company that day was attached to Daniel's brigade, Rodes's division, Ewell's corps. Late in the afternoon, the Union artillery opened up a lengthy barrage, followed by a death-like stillness. On this day, White wrote:

> *'Tis the pause of death—the Angel Azrael for a moment droops his blood-reeking wings and rests on the field of battle.*
>
> *"Make ready, boys—they are charging!" Every man sprang to his post and the enemy come swooping through the woods on our right and in front of Dole's brigade. We pour a few rounds of canister [sic] into their ranks, when we are ordered to.*
>
> *"Cease firing—our men are charging!"*
>
> *A long line of Confederate infantry is seen rapidly advancing towards the enemy's line, and we jump upon the breastworks, loudly cheering them in their supposed charge; but, good Heavens, something is wrong—those Confederates have no muskets! And though 'tis hard to believe, yet a second's glance sufficed to show us that they had surrendered without firing a shot and were going to the Yankee rear as fast as their cowardly legs would carry them. Between that line of Confederates and our battery is one dense mass of Federal infantry, advancing rapidly, and at a trail arms; they were but a short distance from us, but so far to our right that we could not fire into them without killing our own men. Again we sprang to our guns and put in a shot anyway and anywhere we could; but no artillerists could stem the torrent now nor wipe away the foul stain upon the fair banner of Confederate valor. The fourth detachment fights its gun until the first gun is captured, the second gun is captured, the third gun is captured, and its own limber-chest with its No. 6 (Dr. Roberts) captured! Nearly every man in the detachment a recruit—gentlemen recruits, I doff my hat to you!*

Our support was breaking on all sides—on our right and rear the enemy were pouring in upon us in a perfect avalanche. And now comes over us a feeling of sickening horror—not the fear of death, for, so help us God, we thought not of dying, but we thought of the shame in leaving our battery to be captured by the enemy, and that, too, almost without a struggle. Lieutenant Paine, who was standing near the fourth gun, now asked Major Watson, "What must be done?"

I heard Major Watson make no reply, but his countenance was more expressive of dejection, not of fear, for he was the very bravest of men.

Then Major Watson, Lieutenant Reade (our adjutant), Lieutenant Paine, and myself, together with most of the fourth detachment, sprang over the breastworks towards the enemy's main line, and moving obliquely to the left reentered our lines somewhere near the Second Howitzers. Everything was in the direst confusion—all company organization was entirely broken up. Our men, being ordered to take care of themselves, got out of the enemy's way as best they could, scarcely any two of them going together, consequently I am unable to keep any account of their movements; the reader will therefore excuse the seeming egotism if I record my own adventures for the balance of the day.

Time, about 5 P.M. When Major Watson left I concluded it was time for me to be moving, so I sprang over the breastworks also, and as I did so I hung my foot in a root or twig and came down upon the ground with a heavy thwack; then I heard one of my bosom friends say, "There goes poor Buck," but he didn't stop to see whether I had gone or not, and I reckon I would have done as much for him. However, I gallantly picked myself up and made very good time; I thought I was wounded, too; then going some fifty yards to the left I reentered our lines.

In rear of the Third Company was a line of hastily constructed earthworks, occupied by five companies of North Carolina's infantry, belonging to Daniel's brigade, who had been moved from the main line in the morning, we taking their place, and I thought this small body of men would be a nucleus on which we would rally our broken line. So taking an Enfield rifle, cartridge box, etc., from a demoralized infantryman, I made for that line as soon as possible, and there found General Ewell, with several staff officers, endeavoring to rally our men. Several of our boys fall in with these five companies and Ewell orders a charge—five companies to charge as many thousand Yankees; but we do it—we advance with a "yell" and even reach our caissons, but the enemy are too strong for us and we are literally wiped out. It looked to me as if not so many as a dozen got back.

The enemy had not formed a regular line of battle, but seemed to me to be in as much confusion as we were. Private J.M. Fourquean, of our company, is wounded in this charge. Gallant Dick Ewell remains at his post and is manfully endeavoring to bring up the stragglers—it is getting about twilight. By Ewell's side, astraddle of a little pony, is a boy soldier of not over eleven or twelve years of age, and I may live to be a hundred years of age, but I will never forget that little boy—his pony rearing up and pawing in the direction of the enemy, and the gallant little soldier firing his tiny pocket pistol as earnestly as Murat heading a charge.

We reform again, and by this time a brigade, marching by the right flank, comes sweeping down the lines.

"By the left flank!" comes from some old veteran; that swings them into "line of battle," and we knew something had to give way. "Charge, men!—General Lee is looking on!"

With a yell and a dash we made another attempt; this time the Yankees have formed their line, and we get into the closest quarters it was ever, before or since, my fortune to witness. At one time the lines of battle were not over twenty yards apart. The color-bearer falls; private W.E. Goode, of our company, bears them onward. This time we are more successful, and we rush undismayed on the Yankee forces. The fire flashing from their muskets lighted with a bright red glow the faces of our men charging, and upon each man's countenance is seen the determination to win back those guns or else lose his life in the attempt. In the twilight's soft gloaming is seen the form of man against man engaged in fearful death struggling—the yell of determination is heard far above the crash of musketry, whilst ever and anon the discordant note of some wailing victim grates harshly upon the ear as the death ball crashes through the bone.

It is my opinion that it takes a better, braver and cooler man to stand by his "piece" during an engagement than it does to charge any line of battle ever formed, and for this reason: An artillerist has no excitement in his fighting, and frequently is standing up entirely unprotected, apparently doing nothing, simply holding his thumb upon the cannon vent, but if he takes his thumb off that vent a moment too soon he kills the man in front of him.

In an infantry charge every man feels the individuality of his efficiency, and, all fear being subservient to the animal magnetism of excitement, he in reality knows no fear. In the charge I noticed a Federal Major endeavoring to make his men follow him; he was but a few paces off from me; I fired, he fell, and he was so close to me that I got his hat before he fell to the ground. I stopped to load my rifle—a greasy-looking North Carolinian stepped out of ranks, turned him over, took out of his pockets his watch, money, etc., and went on in the charge.

On we pressed until the enemy was driven from our battery, and once more the Confederate flag was floating over the Third Company Richmond Howitzers. From every gun our men had carried off the implements, and that is the reason they had not been turned upon us.

The enemy still hold a portion of our lines, especially a traverse some forty or fifty yards on our right—it becomes a difficult matter to dislodge them, nor can we do it without reinforcement: from this traverse they sweep our lines with a terrible enfilading fire. Who can describe our feelings when we regained our guns! Loud cheers rent the air, and each man seemed endowed with a tenfold strength: quickly the canister [sic] is rammed home and our Napoleon does its work.

A week passed, and terrible losses were experienced by both armies at the Mule Shoe near Spotsylvania. An attack on Rodes's division on the eighteenth brought the fourth gun into action again. White's account of that day's fighting included a description of his "feelings" about his Napoleon:

Attack on Rode's [sic] Division, Ewell's Corp
Wednesday, May 18th, Spotsylvania Courthouse
In our front is heard the sound of many voices, even as the rush and roar of many waters—it is the enemy advancing through the woods in our front, and distinctly can we hear their officers giving the words of command and cheering on their men. Our sharpshooters fall back in good order and take position to the left of the fourth gun and about three hundred yards in front of our line: these sharpshooters were the Twenty-first Regiment, Virginia Infantry, and were as game a set of soldiery as ever fought.

On come the enemy, and plainly can we see them debouching from the woods in our front and massing their troops to attack the hill on our right. Our guns are quickly trained upon them and the command "Fire" is given. One by one our guns open upon them and as the thick blue smoke is blown from them we can see the deadly Napoleon shot and the unerring ten-pound rifle ball ploughing through the serried ranks of the astounded enemy. Vainly do they endeavor to press forward—again and again, we break them, and their officers uselessly dash up and down their lines, endeavoring to hurl them upon our works. The dash has been remorselessly extracted from these gala dressed Auger's Heavy artillerists, taken from the works around Washington to reinforce Grant, and in their first fight—they are but food for our gun-powder.

For one hour and a half this kind of fighting continued and every time the enemy formed for a charge we shattered their columns with artillery alone. The fourth gun fired slowly and deliberately—averaging one shot per minute—as its position was the best on the line, and our ammunition in splendid condition, it is presumable that we did fine execution. Finally the enemy, after making another abortive attempt, broke and incontinently fled, leaving us undisturbed masters of the field. Only three men in our company were wounded, two of whom were scarcely hurt, and the other (Private W.C.A. Mayo) not seriously injured. The enemy also attacked our lines farther to the right, in front of Gordon's and Pegram's brigades, and as with us, the artillery broke their lines, driving them back without the assistance of the infantry.

This fight has been most beneficial to us in restoring confidence to our men, for, especially on our part of the line, they have become somewhat discouraged, having suffered so severely.

The "gunner" of the fourth detachment, Corporal Miles H. Gardner, being temporarily attached to the third gun, owing to our severe loss in non-commissioned officers during the engagement of the 10th, I took my old position and acted in his stead. If there be any pleasure in fighting, it is when one is "gunner" of a splendid Napoleon gun, the men working like clock-work, ammunition in splendid order, and no one shooting at you. Such was the fight of to-day.

All journalistic writings are more or less egotistical, and, therefore, I hope the reader will not consider the writer more so than the generality of fallable [sic] *humanity when I say that in hearing Generals, Colonels, Captains, Lieutenants and greasy looking, but indisputably brave privates compliment, in the highest terms, the accuracy of the fire of the "fourth" gun, my heart beat with the proudest throb of emotion that ever it has felt since the commencement of the war. After the fight our infantry hung around the powder-begrimed and heated "Napoleon," patted it affectionately on the breach and muzzle, and made all manner of queer remarks concerning its effectiveness and accuracy. One strapping looking fellow sang out to his comrade, "Look here, Jim—here's our gun! This is the gun we pulled out'n the mud that ar' night."*

And sure enough, it was the same gun. They ever afterwards claimed an ownership in the fourth gun, Third company. The infantrymen all wanted to see the artillery "tricks" (as they called the "implements" with which we worked the gun), and we had to show them the friction primers, lanyard, priming wire, thumb-stall, etc., and also had to explain to them the difference between spherical case shot, shell, and canister. The first named projectile was used by us nearly altogether to-day, and, being a very destructive missile, inflicted terrible injury upon the enemy. Some of us walked down to the position where the enemy, in the morning, had been massing his troops for a "charge," and the most horrible sights we ever witnessed. Our infantry had not fired a shot—all the work had been done by artillery. Few men were simply wounded—nearly all were dead, and literally torn into atoms; some shot through and through by cannon balls, some with arms and legs knocked off, and some with their heads crushed in by the fatal fragments of exploded shell. Horrible, horrible! They left several hundred of their dead in our front, and as it is to be presumed that many were carried off, their loss must have been severe. Our infantry were ordered not to fire until their line of battle got within two hundred yards of our breastworks, and as they did not get that near to us the artillery had it all to themselves. The remaining part of the day was more than usually quiet. General Lee sent us word not only at what time they intended to make the charge, but also what troops would be engaged in it. I think he expected a much heavier fight, for he put the whole of Jackson's old division, much depleted, it is true, to support one detachment of our company (Fourth), and behind that detachment we had three lines of breastworks. It is difficult for us to get good drinking water. Oh, for a good mint julep!

White and his Napoleon continued to do service in the Army of Northern Virginia following Spotsylvania. They were together at North Anna, Polegreen Church and New Market Heights on the north side of the James River. It was altogether appropriate that both the man and his gun were at Appomattox on Sunday, April 9, 1865. White's last entry in his diary read:

A shell comes hurtling down our line—another and another follow fast, and follow faster. Just as cheerfully and just as defiantly as at Bethel, four years ago, when our hopes were big with the fate and fame of a new-born nation, do our boys go forth and meet them and our guns hurl back their shot and shell.

ONE BATTLE, TWO ACCOUNTS

The following two reports of the action at Polegreen Church furnish us
with a vivid picture of how a Confederate and Union soldier participated
in the same battle. Though much of this book has to do with violence of
the worst sort, perhaps the reader will join me in not wishing to do violence
to the literary work of those two soldiers by abbreviating or excising this
particular entry in their diaries. There is clearly the mark of the poet in
Sergeant William S. White's writing of his day at Polegreen. White's diary
entry below is not only an eyewitness account of the destruction of the
church but also the poignant account of the feelings of the man who fired
the shot:

> *Attempt to Force Our Lines at Polegreen Church, Wednesday, June 1ˢᵗ*
> *It was early in the morning, before light, when the fourth gun went into
> position, and it was so dark that I could form no idea of location. This
> gun relieved a piece of artillery belonging to the First Howitzers, under the
> special command of Captain Ed. S. McCarthy, and as I moved in to take
> his place he remarked that I would have a warm time of it, as the Yankee
> skirmishers were almost right up to the gun. Poor fellow, I never saw him
> afterward—moved off to another position and was killed on the 4ᵗʰ. He
> was a brave soldier and an efficient officer, greatly beloved by his company.*
>
> *At daybreak it became quite evident that the fourth gun had gotten into
> a warm place, for the enemy's sharpshooters were swarming around us in
> countless numbers. It is said that Charles Field's division allowed the Yankee
> sharpshooters to get into our line of rifle pits (made for our skirmishers) and
> then were not able to drive them out again; consequently the enemy were so
> close to our works that we dared not put our heads above them.*
>
> *The hot summer's sun poured its blinding rays down upon our unprotected
> heads, not a leaf nor a twig was nigh to shelter us, and the sand became so
> hot that it seemed as if it were molten metal, the sharp whiz of the deadly
> Minie creating the only breath of air stirring. The position of the fourth
> gun was anything but satisfactory to me, occupying, as it did, a redoubt
> thrown up some fifty yards in front of our regular line of earthworks. Our
> skirmish line in front was extremely weak, and was but a stone's throw
> in front of us. The enemy on the left of this gun were much nearer than
> they were in front, and occupied higher ground than we did; consequently
> they could shoot down into our redoubt. Captain McCarthy had in a great
> measure remedied that by raising the left salient of the earthwork. Still we*

were not entirely protected, and this very measure of relief proved of serious disadvantage later in the day.

This morning we were supported by Harry Hays' brigade, Early's division, but about noon William W. Kirkland's brigade, Heth's division, Hill's corps, relieved Hays, and as it was impossible to remove the artillery until nightfall we were ordered to remain until that time. During the change in the disposition of the infantry forces the enemy, noticing the movement, poured a volley or two of musketry into our men, killing and wounding some of Kirkland's brigade. The immediate support of the "left section" of our company, guns No. 3 and 4, was the Eleventh North Carolina infantry; that is, the old Bethel regiment, or what was then the First North Carolina, its number now being changed to the Eleventh. The enemy's sharpshooters having gotten almost within a stone's throw of our breastworks, annoyed us terribly. Soldiers, even in the most trying hours, will have their sport, and some of us would take off our greasy-looking caps, set them up on sticks, and hold them above the redoubt just to see how near the Yankees could come to them.

A sudden volley of musketry from our skirmishers warned us that the time for amusement had passed and the moment for work had arrived—on, on the blue line comes, like a wave from the heaving ocean it sweeps with resistless force. But there is a barrier to stem that swelling tide, a rugged rock to roll back that seething stream, a Hill to climb, a Heth to pass, and forth from the Confederate lines dart a stream of fire from brazen-mouthed Napoleons, all charged with murderous grape.

And as the sound of men's voices rose above the din and confusion of ensanguined strife a stream of fire rises from the roof of that old time-honored house of worship, the church of my ancestors, the church of Samuel Davies—Pole Green, perhaps the oldest Presbyterian church in Virginia—set on fire by a shot from my own gun.

My thoughts, even [a]mid the din and confusion of battle, flew backward to childhood's bright and sunny days—aye, to days of merry boyhood, and I remembered that in Pole Green my own father received his Christian name; that there my ancestors had worshipped the true God, and that for many, many years it had been connected with the dearest annals of the Presbyterian Church—now it was passing away in the red glare of war.

As those flames flickered and glared and cast their lurid lights full into the faces of those Southrons [sic] struggling for all most dear to men, a new, a stronger spirit of endurance seemed given them, and ere the mouldering [sic] embers were shedding their dying halo, the enemy were driven back, and victory, once more, was ours.

The enemy, coming up upon the left of the fourth gun, it was sometime before we could get a fair shot at them. It will be remembered that the fourth gun was some distance in front of the main line, occupying a single redoubt, and, in order to protect the cannoniers from the enemy's skirmishers, occupying on our left higher ground than we did, our left salient was heightened so we could not fire over it. They charged in line of battle, but, for some reason, changed into column—the head of the column was not over twenty yards from the muzzle of the fourth gun, double charged with canister, when we fired the first shot. When using canister the flame from the gun seems to go much farther than when using any other projectile, and it looked to me as if the flame from our gun ran half way down their line. We fired seventeen rounds of canister into that column and its advance was stopped. Lieutenant Carter, seeing this charge before we did, he being stationed some distance to our right, and thinking we were asleep, sent a cannonier to wake us up. We could not fire any sooner, but when we did get to work we went in a hurry. An officer told me that we fired the first eleven shots in one minute. Our boys showed no signs of wavering, but stood firmly to their posts and made the "prettiest fight" on record.

The enemy were charging at "a right shoulder shift," and did not fire at all. Many a blue coated Federal was left on the field, and a good number came into our lines, surrendering. Three years ago a band of youthful artillerists went forth from their native city to meet the invading foeman. With scarcely an exception none of them had reached the sterner years of manhood, and yet they went forth to conquer or to die. Beardless faces and merry blue eyes were among them; the elastic step and the buoyancy of youth betokened the will to be and to make brave soldiers of our brave and beautiful metropolis. How proudly they marched through the wide streets of noble old Richmond, and she, as if proud of her gallant sons, sent forth her daughters fair to bid them stand like the sturdy yeomanry of old or else come back to her never again!

At Bethel those youthful soldiers drove back and defeated United States regulars—here on one side was a band of schoolboys handling their artillery with a coolness and consummate skill that veterans would have gloried in, and on the other side regulars fought for pay and for the upholding of a Government that had become unbearable to over eight millions of souls.

A gallant regiment of North Carolina infantry, led by the dauntless D.H. Hill, of whom "Stonewall" Jackson said: "He is the very bravest man I ever knew," supported those boy-artillerists and won for itself a name that will last so long as men remember gallant deeds. 'Twas then that the glad shout first rang through the air that the sons of a new-born

Confederacy had gained a great, a glorious victory! But, alas! this was only the commencement of the great struggle—other and more bloody battles were yet to be fought, and countless thousands of brave and gallant men were yet to fall. The bloody sun of Death had scarcely arisen—the noontide of destruction was not yet.

Three years afterward that company of boy-artillerists, now "grown old in wars," stand side by side with that same Carolina regiment and face the charging foeman!

The company is sadly changed now, for many who fought with us then sleep in the soldier's grave—some fell at Charlestown, some at Fredericksburg, some at Chancellorsville, some at Gettysburg, thirty-nine were lost to us at Spotsylvania Courthouse, and many stand with the Third Company now who were strangers to us then. The old First North Carolina is vastly changed too, for where are the thirteen hundred men who landed at Yorktown in '61?

Ask the pale moon if she ever has seen any of those gallant missing ones stretched full length on the red field of battle?

Ask the stormy winds if ever they have blown rudely over the graves of those gallant Carolinians whose places are now vacant in that brave old regiment?

Ah, winds! blow softly, reverently over the graves of those that are missing from that dear old regiment, for they are answering the reveille in that army whose Captain is the Son of God. He who was Colonel D.H. Hill then now wears the wreath of a General, and well worthy is he to wear it; its Lieutenant-Colonel now sleeps in the soldier's grave; its Major is a Brigadier-General now; and one of its officers, Robert Hoke, then an almost unknown Captain, a few weeks since returned from Carolina's coast wearing an evergreen garland of victory entwined on Plymouth's field, and the stars of a Division-General are his reward. (Perhaps you think this is a general hoax).

The enemy, after having failed in our front, tried the strength of our lines a short distance to our right, but two far away for us to render any assistance. For a time, the firing was quite heavy, but we repulsed them easily, and the night of the 1ˢᵗ of June ended another brilliant day to our arms. After dark, all became quiet, and our company was relieved by a battery from Hill's corps—we retiring to the rear. Griffin's four Napoleon guns, on our left, did fine execution. Lieutenant Dinguid and one other killed. No one was hurt in the Third company, but many narrow escapes were made.

James Aubery was one of four brothers who enlisted in the Union army on the same day in Vermont. As the war wore on, they became separated in service, James becoming a sergeant in the Thirty-sixth Wisconsin Infantry. Following the war, he wrote the history of his regiment, based on his diary and existing military records of the unit. (See Chapter 4.)

In his account of the battle at Polegreen on June 1, he has confused Polegreen Church with Bethesda, which was on down the long line toward Cold Harbor. In fact, the extreme left of Hancock's Second Corps (Gibbon's division), on the afternoon of June 1, was no closer than a mile and a half to Bethesda Church. Warren's Fifth Corps was still at Bethesda on the first. The ten companies of the Thirty-sixth Wisconsin Volunteer Infantry were sent into battle at Polegreen on this afternoon. In midafternoon, the word had come down and quickly disseminated that Hancock's corps would be withdrawn after dark for an all-night march to Cold Harbor. They would follow the same route of Wright's corps, which had moved the night before. They were expected to be in position to fight the next day, June 2. Before leaving, however, they would make a "demonstration" by an attack, not an all-out battle, on Lee's left flank. James Aubery gave his account of the fight. Referring to the orders to move at dark, he wrote:

> From these orders, evidently, we were preparing to move again on the enemy's flank, but before we were to move it was destined that we have a "parting shot," which before we got through, made out to be a historical battle, placing us nearly at the head of the Three Hundred Fighting Regiments in casualties. From my diary I take the following, which is also in the Adjutant-General's Report, State of Wisconsin:
>
> On the 1ˢᵗ of June occurred the battle of Totopotomoy (or Bethesda Church), a general engagement along various parts of the line. About 4 in the afternoon, the line four miles to the left being very severely pressed by the enemy, orders were received for a vigorous demonstration in front of the First Brigade, in order to restrain the rebel division which were [sic] moving to reinforce their [sic] line to the left. Four companies on the right of the regiment (B, E, F, G) under command of Captain Warner were moved forward as skirmishers, forming part of the line which was to advance. The rebels held a strong line of works, with guns mounted, about one hundred yards to the front, to reach which it was necessary to cross an open field. At the command to advance, these companies moved forward at double quick. The line at the right and left, composed of veterans, after advancing a few rods and firing one volley, fell back to the works. The enemy opened

upon the advancing line with grape, and very severe musketry from the front with oblique fire from right and left, making it almost impossible for a man to live on the field. The line continued to advance, driving in the rebel skirmishers, a portion of it actually passing down and over the rebel works. Of two hundred and forty men of the Thirty-sixth engaged in the charge, one hundred and forty were killed, wounded or taken prisoners. While this seemed like a useless sacrifice of life, it fully accomplished the object proposed. The rebel divisions were returned to this part of the line on a double quick, and our line of the left, already hard pressed, was thus enabled to maintain its ground. In the charge, Captain Burwell, a brave and efficient officer, was mortally wounded and taken prisoner. Captain Lindley was slightly wounded and Lieutenant Newton severely wounded and taken prisoner. The other six companies while advancing lost about fifty men wounded.

During this whole day there was much maneuvering along our whole line, preparing for what soon came, as will be seen by the orders of our commanders. I only take a few pertaining to our direct command. This was one of our "busiest" days and cut into our numbers, bringing the regiment down to compare with the veteran regiments. There were some very trying experiences by some of those who were wounded and crawled off the field, which I will speak of later.

When the action described by Aubery is seen in the light of these troops having been in combat only fourteen days, it is not difficult to imagine the shocking impact on those young men. Their first experience in battle had occurred on May 19. At Polegreen, they began to earn the title of being near the top of the list of the "Three Hundred Fighting Regiments" with the most casualties.

George Haw's Story

Sometime during this period, one of the four Haw brothers who served in the Confederate army, George Pitman Haw, found himself in the midst of an interesting incident. The exact date of this is difficult to tell, as one attempts to put together the pieces of this account. Immediately after Lincoln called for troops to enforce the Union and Virginia seceded, George Haw enlisted in the Hanover Grays. Within a month, he was seeing action in the line and later, at Sharpsburg, lost an arm. In telling of his war experience, he wrote of an incident that occurred later when Grant was moving through Hanover County:

> As soon as I was sufficiently cured, I was put on light duty and made an Enrolling Officer. My career in the field ceased then. After that, when occasion offered, I went with some of the soldiers following up the raid, when it passed through my country, and was several times under fire, and one time when Grant's Army was in Hanover, I passed through Pole Green Church, and went through the line and beyond the farthest picket, to my father's residence, and within 100 or 200 yards of their house, in the effort to get in touch with my two younger brothers and bring them out. I got to the public road which runs in front of my father's house about 100 yards distant, and as I was about to go into the road I saw a Yankee soldier walking leisurely down the road, and I drew my pistol and debated with myself whether I would capture him or not. But I concluded that as I was beyond our line, it would be a rather dangerous experiment for me, a one-armed man, to undertake to carry that fellow to our lines safely. I afterwards learned that he had just deserted his own army, and gave himself up a few miles further to our picket. I uncocked my pistol, went back to my house and returned to Pole Green Church, and slept on the ground that night with the picket.
>
> The next morning, soon after daylight, I returned to my father's house where I had a talk with my mother and instructed her to send my brothers to meet me. And I stood in her yard and looked at the Cavalry pickets, about 400 or 500 yards from her house, looking in my direction. I then returned, waited until my brothers came up and together we returned to Richmond and told them that I had been to my father's house which was five miles nearer the Yankee line than our line was.
>
> General Tom Rosser asked me if I had seen the army's pickets. I said I had seen none. He then put his men in movement and went to where I told him I had been. When he got to my father's house he ran the Yankees away from the place. They had killed and were cutting up the last cow my father had when he drove them away.

The time required for the unfolding of these events would make it extremely difficult for them to have occurred between the posting of the Confederate picket at Polegreen on May 28 and Grant's occupation north of the Totopotomoy on May 29 and for the next several days around the Haw home. The event could have happened after Grant's right wing had been sent down to Cold Harbor. But if this happened, why didn't Haw mention that the church building was in ashes when he slept with the picket there? His account was written many years later, and that may be the answer. It is true that Heth's division and Confederate cavalry were still in the Polegreen area for several days after the Totopotomoy main action had ended, and some fighting took place at Haw's Shop on June 3.

DESTITUTION IN HANOVER COUNTY

It might be wondered why old Polegreen Church was never rebuilt after the war. Here was a church that, for over one hundred years, had stood as a symbol of one of the most important chapters in the common history shared by the North and South and a reminder of one of the most remarkable men in eighteenth-century colonial America, Samuel Davies. The answer is really not that difficult to understand. The congregation at Polegreen had dwindled in size considerably long before the Civil War began. For about fifty years, it had shared the same minister with Salem Church near Haw's Shop. Thomas Williamson Hooper was destined to be the last pastor of the United Church of Salem and Polegreen. After the destruction of Polegreen on June 2, 1864, the members of the church who wished traveled the extra four miles on down to Haw's Shop to worship.

One of the major reasons the church was not rebuilt was the destitute condition of its members. Not many counties of the country, North or South, were fought over as much as Hanover. The campaign of 1864 was much worse than that of 1862. By '64, the evolving strategy of the Federal high command was clearly established. The South was to be defeated by whatever means possible, including confiscation and destruction of civilian property and resources. Sheridan's Valley Campaign tactics were employed wherever possible, including the campaign from the Rapidan to Petersburg. The invading army was to live off the land as much as it could, for the obvious reasons—to demoralize the civilian population and make it as difficult as possible to supply the Southern forces.

Joseph Q. Haw, of the Haw's Shop family, reflecting on the fortunes of his own kin and the condition of many of his Hanover County neighbors, described the kind of situation faced by many Southern families:

> *When the Haw boys volunteered and entered the Southern army, Haw's Shop was closed down, as nearly all of the white employees entered the service. It was*

suggested that the machinery be moved to Richmond and that John Haw have the men detailed and manufacture ammunition for the government. To this his sons would not agree, as it was thought by the men at the front to be cowardly to serve in what were called "bombproof" positions. Realizing that this valuable property would be destroyed by the enemy, John Haw, after McClellan had retired, sold it to the Tredegar Works of Richmond. Failing to invest the money in valuable real estate or other sound property, it was a total loss.

THE THIRTY-SIXTH WISCONSIN MONUMENT

Charles A. Storke was sixteen years old on the morning of June 1, 1864, when he and his comrades of the Thirty-sixth Wisconsin Volunteer Infantry were camped in a ravine behind Polegreen Presbyterian Church in Hanover County. It was a scorching hot day, and the relief offered by the presence of the nearby spring was a godsend. Dryness of mouth caused by the heat was intensified at noon by the news that the Thirty-sixth Wisconsin was going to go into battle at 4:30 p.m. The regiment had been in active combat duty for only two weeks. The late afternoon charge was designed to tie down the Rebel force on the left wing of its defense line along the Totopotomoy Creek.

Companies B, E, F and G were to lead the charge in the face of Breckinridge's men, who were backed up by artillery of Hardaway's battalion. The men of the Thirty-sixth came up the steep slope from the ravine through the woods and emerged into an open field. Four hundred yards to the southwest could be clearly seen the main earthwork battle line of the Confederates. The order to advance was given, and a wild charge toward the enemy ensued. Storke and 239 of his companions raced ahead. Exposure to musket and cannon fire was total. The man next to him in the frantic charge was destroyed by a cannonball. The sixteen-year-old suddenly found himself at the foot of the Confederate earthwork. He scrambled over it, rolled into the depression beside Confederate artillery, leaped to his feet, dashed across Shady Grove Church (now Polegreen) Road and fell exhausted within a pine thicket. Too much was happening in front of the Confederate line to allow for any pursuit of the young man into the woods.

Charles Storke, close to exhaustion, fell behind a fallen log, motionless, and listened to the battle rage. As the fighting died down and dusk approached, he entertained the idea he might slip back through the lines after dark, but it was not to be. Suddenly, he heard the snap of a twig and the rustle of leaves. He turned his head and stared into the barrel of a Confederate musket. Storke later recalled the first intelligible words he had heard for three hours: "Get up, you damn Yankee. I gotcha cuvvered."

From June 1, 1864, until the end of the war, Storke was a prisoner. He was taken first into Richmond to the Pemberton Building across the street from Libby Prison. From there, he was sent to Andersonville. As Sherman advanced through Georgia to the sea, Andersonville was emptied, and Storke was sent to Savannah and then Millen, Blackshire and Florence military prisons. Finally, he was discharged in December 1865 in Madison, Wisconsin.

Of the 240 men of the four companies that charged across that open field on June 1, every fifth man was killed, seven out of ten wounded and thirty-nine taken prisoner.

Storke entered a Kalamazoo, Michigan college after the war, studied for three years, transferred to Cornell University as a junior and graduated with honors in 1870. After teaching at Adelphi College in Brooklyn, New York, for two years, he accepted a teaching position at Santa Barbara College in California. In 1873, he moved to Los Angeles and founded the *Los Angeles Herald* newspaper. In later years, Storke practiced law successfully.

Storke was drawn back to the scene of his wartime adventure and visited the site of the battle near Polegreen Church. He is quoted in General Orders XI (1924–25) of the Grand Army of the Republic, Department of Nevada and California, stating his reasons for erecting the ten-foot granite monument in Hanover County. When Storke came to Virginia for the last time in 1924 for the dedication of the monument, he remarked:

> *I came to Virginia in 1910. I came the second and third times and always I was not satisfied because I could do nothing for my comrades who had died. I tried to look up their graves and could not find a trace of them. I determined then to put up a monument where they had received their wounds. I secured an acre of ground near Shelton House within 20 feet of where I was captured in 1864.*

The inscription on the monument reads as follows: "This monument has been erected by one of their comrades, Charles A. Storke, in memory of the members of Companies B, E, F, and G of the Thirty-Sixth Wisconsin Volunteer Infantry who fought here on the 1st day of June 1864." Storke returned with his granddaughter in 1924 for the dedication of the monument on the one-acre site. He promptly deeded the property, with improvements, to Hanover County, Virginia, which is now responsible for the upkeep of the memorial to the young men from Wisconsin who were killed, wounded or imprisoned.

The monument on Route 627 is the only Union marker outside a national cemetery in central Virginia.

The Last Parade

They thronged the streets of this old town when [Milledge L.] Bonham brought his volunteers with their Palmetto flag in 1861. They cheered the lads who took up arms when first Virginia called. With doubtful glance they looked upon the men who hailed from New Orleans, the "Tigers" of the Bayou state. When [James] Longstreet led his veterans from Centreville to hold the Yorktown line, all Richmond brought out food and draped the bayonets. When first the city heard the distant growl of Union guns, each regiment that came to strengthen [General Robert E.] Lee was welcomed as the savior of the South. The long procession of the carts that brought a groaning load across the Chickahominy from Gaines' Mill was watched with aching hearts.

Another year and solemn strains and mourning drums received the train that had the silent form of him who was the "right arm" of his famous chief. That was the darkest day, save one, that Richmond ever knew, for when the "Stonewall" fell, the stoutest bulwark of the South was down. With Jackson dead, where was another such?

When [George E.] Pickett's soldiers came, a shattered fragment of defiant wrath, to tell how hell itself had opened on that hill [ridge] at Gettysburg, the townsfolk gazed as if on men who had upturned their graves. The months that followed saw a steady flow into the mills of death. Each night the sleeping street was wakened by the tread of veterans who hurried on to meet the sullen [Major General George G.] Meade or hastened back to check the wily [Major General Philip H.] Sheridan. The clatter of the horses' hoofs, the rumble of the trains, the drum at dawn, the bugle on the midnight air—all these the leaguered city heard till children's talk was all of arms, and every chat across the garden wall was punctuated by the sound of fratricidal strife.

Ten months of thunder and of ceaseless march and then the end. Brave Custis Lee led out the last defenders of the town, and limping [Richard S.] Ewell rode away while flames leaped up and bridges burned and Trojan women waited death. The next parade was set to fastest time, as up the hill and past St. Paul's and in the gates the Federals rode and tore with wildest cheers the still-defiant flag from off the capitol. Dark orgy in the underworld and brutish plunder of the stores, a wider stretch of fire, the mad rejoicing of the slaves, the sly emergence of the spies; and after that the slow return of one gray rider through the wreck of flames and dreams, a solitary horseman on a weary steed, with only youth and age to pay him homage as he stopped before his door and bowed to all and climbed the steps and went within and put aside his blade to work for peace.

Excited days of preparation then, and pontoons thrown across the James. The army of the victor, [U.S.] Grant, the gossips said, was soon to march through Richmond and see the ashes of the pinnacles on which its distant gaze had long been fixed. They came. In endless lines, all day they moved, all night, until the city's tearful folk became bewildered in their count and asked, How could the "thin, gray line" have stood so long against that host?

At last the blue-coats left and civil rule returned, in poverty and pain, but with a memory that made the humblest rich. The fallen walls were raised again, the peaceful smoke of busy trade rose where the battle-fumes had hung. For twenty years, the soldiers of the South remained behind the counter or the plow, until the day when [Joseph E.] Johnston led them out to lay the cornerstone of what the South designed to be a fit memorial to the matchless Lee. A few years more, and when the figure stood upon the pedestal, the word went out that every man who wore the gray should muster in the ranks again and pass before the chieftain on old Traveller. A day that was when love became the meat of life!

Reunions multiplied. A grateful city gladly threw its portals wide each time the aged survivors of Homeric strife returned to view the scenes of youth. A deep emotion rose as [Bedford] Forrest's troopers galloped past and Texans raised the "rebel yell." Today the city has its last review. The armies of the South will march our streets no more. It is the rear guard, engaged with death, that passes now. Who that remembers other days can face that truth and still withhold his tears? The dreams of youth have faded in the twilight of the years. The deeds that shook a continent belong to history. Farewell; sound taps! And then a generation new must face its battles in its turn, forever heartened by that heritage.

"The Last Parade" is an editorial by Douglas Southall Freeman printed in the Richmond News Leader *of Friday, June 24, 1932, the last day of the forty-second annual reunion of the United Confederate Veterans. It is reprinted here by permission of the Douglas S. Freeman Foundation.*

Bibliography

MAPS

"The Battle-Field of Totopotomoy, Virginia." Plate 46 in *The Official Military Atlas of the Civil War*. Compiled by Calvin S. Cowles. New York: Fairfax Press, 1983.

"The Battlefields of the Totopotomoy and Bethesda Church, Virginia." Plate 55 in *The Official Military Atlas of the Civil War*. Compiled by Calvin S. Cowles. New York: Fairfax Press, 1983.

Campbell, A.H., "Battlefields of Hanover County," n.d. Copy in Richmond National Battlefield Park (NBP) files.

"Hanover County, Va., 1864" in Jeremy F. Gilmer Collection, Virginia Historical Society, Richmond.

Henderson, D.E. Untitled sketch map, n.d. Copy in Richmond NBP files.

Lowe, David. "Military Earthworks Surviving in the Vicinity of Totopotomoy Creek, Virginia." Cultural Resources GIS, National Park Service, Washington, D.C., September 1999. Copy in Richmond NBP files.

"Map from Maj. A.H. Campbell's Surveys." Plate 81 in *The Official Military Atlas of the Civil War*. Compiled by Calvin S. Cowles. New York: Fairfax Press, 1983.

Sketch map prepared by the Engineer Department, Army of the Potomac (U.S.), May 30, 1864. Copy in Richmond NBP files.

PRIMARY SOURCES

Alexander, Edward Porter. Diary, May–June 1864. Alexander Papers, Southern Historical Collection, University of North Carolina, Chapel Hill.

————. *Fighting for the Confederacy: The Personal Recollections of General Edward Porter Alexander*. Edited by Gary W. Gallagher. Chapel Hill: University of North Carolina Press, 1989, 395–96.

Billings, John D. *The History of the Tenth Massachusetts Battery*. Boston: Arakelyan Press, 1909, 251–55.

Cadwallander, James M. Diary, May 1864. Copy in Richmond NBP files.

Cockrell, Monroe F., ed. *Gunner with Stonewall: Reminiscences of William Thomas Poague*. Wilmington, NC: Broadfoot Publishing Co., 1989, 95–6.

Dame, William M. *From the Rapidan to Richmond and the Spotsylvania Campaign*. Baltimore, MD: Green Lucas, 1920, 191–92.

Dowdey, Clifford, and Louis H. Manarin, eds. *The Wartime Papers of R.E. Lee*. Boston: Little, Brown & Co., 1961, 754–55.

Early, Jubal A. *Jubal Early's Memoirs*. Baltimore, MD: Nautical & Aviation Publishing Co. of America, 1989, 361–62.

Griffin, Charles A. Diary, May–June 1864. Copy in Richmond NBP files.

Hewitt, Janet B., et al., eds. *Supplement to the Official Records of the Union and Confederate Armies*. Vol. 6, part 1. Wilmington, NC: Broadfoot Publishing Co., 1996, 708, 751. Includes the reports of Confederate officers involved in the Totopotomoy operations.

History Committee. *History of the Nineteenth Regiment Massachusetts Volunteer Infantry*. Salem, MA: Salem Press Co., 1906, 317.

Marsh, W.B., and Lewis H. Steiner. Journal, May–June 1864. Copy in Richmond NBP files.

McIntosh, D.G. Description of 1911 visit to Richmond area. Mcintosh Papers, Virginia Historical Society, Richmond.

McMurran, Joseph. Diary, May–June 1864. Library of Virginia, Richmond.

Mills, George H. *History of the Sixteenth North Carolina Regiment in the Civil War*. Hamilton, NY: Edmonston Publishing Inc., 1992, 54.

Powell, William H. *The Fifth Army Corps*. Dayton, OH: Press of Morningside Bookshop, 1984, 664–71.

Purifoy, John. *History of the Jeff Davis Artillery*, p. 243, excerpt in Richmond NBP files.

Runge, William H., ed. *Four Years in the Confederate Artillery: The Diary of Private Henry Robinson Berkeley*. Chapel Hill: University of North Carolina Press, 1961, 78.

Thomas, James W. Diary, May–June 1864. Copy in Richmond NBP files.

U.S. War Department. *The War of the Rebellion: The Official Records of the Union and Confederate Armies*. Vol. 36, part 1. Washington, D.C.: Government Printing Office, 1884, 343–44, 371, 381–82, 399, 511–12, 543, 564–65, 688, 913, 951–52, 674, 726, 734, 739. Includes the reports of many Federal officers who were involved with the Totopotomoy operations.

Wainwright, Charles S. *A Diary of Battle: The Personal Journals of Colonel Charles S. Wainwright 1861–1865*. Edited by Allen Nevins. New York: Harcourt, Brace & World Inc., 1962, 392–94, 396.

Walker, Charles N., and Rosemary Walker, eds. "Diary of the War by Robt. S. Robertson." *Old Fort News* 28, no. 4: 197–203.

Walker, Francis A. *History of the Second Army Corps*. New York: Charles Scribner's Sons, 1887, 499–500, 502–03.

Worsham, John H. *One of Jackson's Foot Cavalry*. Jackson, TN: McCowat-Mercer Press Inc., 1964, 143.

SECONDARY SOURCES

Baltz, Louis J. *The Battle of Cold Harbor*. Lynchburg, VA: H.E. Howard Inc., 1994.

Furgurson, Ernest B. *Not War But Murder*. New York: Alfred A. Knopf, 2000.

Hanover County Historical Society. *Old Homes of Hanover County, Virginia*. Hanover, VA: Hanover County Historical Society, 1983.

Index

S

T

W

About the Author

Douglas Southall Freeman (1886–1953), Pulitzer Prize–winning biographer and renowned editor of the *Richmond (VA) News Leader*, characterized his heroes with one word. For Robert E. Lee, his word was "duty." Admirers of Dr. Robert Bluford Jr. might consider choosing the word "tireless."

Bob, a Richmond native, interrupted his studies for the ministry at Hampden-Sydney College in May 1942 to volunteer for the U.S. Army Air Force. He served as a B-24 bomber pilot and squadron leader in the Eighth Air Force during World War II and then returned to Hampden-Sydney, where he graduated in 1947 as valedictorian. He subsequently graduated, cum laude, from Union Theological Seminary in Richmond in 1950 and earned graduate degrees from the seminary in 1954 and 1957. In the 1950s, he also served as campus minister at Virginia Polytechnic Institute and in pastorates in North Carolina and South Carolina.

He was active in the civil rights movement on campuses in the 1960s and in peaceful protests of U.S. military involvement in Southeast Asia. In 1971, Bob was a cofounder of the Fan Free Medical Clinic in Richmond. He served on the board of directors of Planned Parenthood in Richmond. Over the last forty years, he has served as minister or associate at Presbyterian churches in Richmond and currently, at ninety-five, is still active as a pastor and preacher.

During his ministry, he served as a leader and volunteer in projects to preserve numerous historic sites in Virginia, including two—the Historic Polegreen Church Foundation in Hanover County and the Laurel Historic District in Henrico—that were placed on the National Register of Historic Places. He was director of the Douglas Southall Freeman Branch of the Association for the Preservation of Virginia Antiquities. Since 1990, he also has been active with the United Indians of Virginia's efforts to recover nearly two thousand skeletal remains of their ancestors from the Smithsonian Institute. He was elected to the United Indians' board of directors in 1995 and is the only non-Indian to be recognized as a board member.

Since 1989, he has devoted time and energy to the Historic Polegreen Church Foundation. Bob Bluford was recognized "for his determined preservation of the Polegreen meetinghouse site" as the Virginia recipient of the 2004 First Freedom Award bestowed by the Council for America's First Freedom.

In 2011, the Virginia Press Association named Bob "Virginian of the Year." In 2013, the Civil War Preservation Trust, the largest Civil War battlefield preservation association in America, named Bob the recipient of the Edwin C. Bearrs Lifetime Achievement Award.

Written by Jerry Finch, retired ombudsman of the *Richmond Times Dispatch* and former managing editor of the *Richmond News Leader*.